# Enjoy Emotional Freedom

# Enjoy Emotional Freedom

## Simple techniques for living life to the full

Steve Wells M.Psych and Dr David Lake

EXISLE
PUBLISHING

First published 2010

Exisle Publishing Limited
'Moonrising', Narone Creek Road, Wollombi, NSW 2325, Australia
P.O. Box 60–490, Titirangi, Auckland 0642, New Zealand
www.exislepublishing.com

The authors and publisher have made every effort to insure that all information was correct at the time of going to print. However, it should be noted that the retirement of Gary Craig, the creator of EFT, may in the future impact on the availability of training videos and other information from his website, www.emofree.com.

Some content in the early chapters of this book was first published in *Pocket Guide to Emotional Freedom* by Steve Wells & David Lake, Waterford Publishing, 2001.

National Library of Australia Cataloguing-in-Publication Data:

Lake, David, Dr.

Enjoy emotional freedom : simple techniques for living life
to the full / David Lake, Steve Wells.

ISBN 9781921497483 (pbk.)

Includes index.
Bibliography

Emotions.
Stress management.

Wells, Steve.

152.4

Cover and typsetting by Darian Causby, Highway 51 Design Works
Internal illustrations by Shaan Coutinho, Watermark Designs
Typeset in 12/18 Goudy
Printed in Singapore by KHL Printing Co Pte Ltd

This book uses paper sourced under ISO 14001 guidelines from well-managed forests and other controlled sources.

10 9 8 7 6 5 4 3

*For Louise, Josh, Olivia and Callum. I love you always*
STEVE WELLS

*For Gerry and her affectionate smile. Love and acceptance always*
DAVID LAKE

# Contents

# Introduction

This book will give you an introduction to two innovative and exciting personal change techniques from the new and rapidly expanding field of Energy Psychology. These techniques — Emotional Freedom Techniques (EFT) and Simple Energy Techniques (SET) — enable you to become free from the limiting effects of negative emotions in your life. These revolutionary tools, which have been exciting health and healing professionals around the world, are now available to ordinary people who can use them to gain relief from everyday emotional problems and bodily tensions.

Sadly, all too often negative emotions such as fear, hurt, guilt and anger intrude on our ability to lead an effective and fulfilling life. These emotions affect most of us on a daily basis, causing us to say and do things we regret, or keep us from doing the things we'd like to do. In a quest to be free from the toxic effects of these negative emotions, many people turn to food, drugs, alcohol and a whole range of self-destructive behaviours, all of which inevitably end up reinforcing negative patterns and restricting personal happiness.

However, you don't have to be trapped in old, destructive patterns anymore. You can now free yourself by using the personal change techniques described in this book. These simple approaches will give you calm and balance and help you to start resolving any issues of tension, stress and poor balance in your body. These special treatments have the potential to guide you, to act as a 'safety net', and to take care of any unhelpful or hurtful negative reactions you may experience. Willpower is good, but it won't last unless there is an emotional change as well. The same goes for changing your way of thinking: without a corresponding emotional change, a change in thinking is usually short-lived. With these new tools for emotional freedom, you will be able to tackle any problem areas where your thinking and your actions have previously not managed to produce a positive result.

During our extensive careers in medical and psychological consultancy, we have both witnessed the life-affirming and healing effects of these techniques. Together, they are the most useful and practical techniques that we have encountered, and they have given us the most personal and professional satisfaction. Combine this with the other tips and techniques featured in this book and you can get the results you want with far less stress than ever before. To help you even more, we also conduct training programs and workshops worldwide, both for professionals and members of the public. (Please see Appendix 4: Further Reading at the end of the book for details.)

This book explains everything you need to know to get started using these new Energy Techniques. It is designed as a handy resource you can consult as needed. We expect you will return to it often and gain the emotional freedom you've been searching for. We hope you enjoy the journey.

# Important Note

This book provides information on Emotional Freedom Techniques (EFT) and Simple Energy Techniques (SET) in an effort to expand the use of these techniques around the world. While SET was developed by the authors, the information on EFT which is included in this book represents the ideas and innovations of the authors only and not those of Gary Craig, the creator of EFT. Complete understanding of EFT and the EFT training videos, as originally taught by Gary Craig, are available at www.emofree.com.

## Disclaimer

All the treatments and advice described in this book are meant for self-help purposes only, and do not necessarily imply that everyone will benefit, or be cured, solely by their own efforts. *It is important to remember that these are **techniques** only, and not therapies in themselves.*

While in practice the outcomes of EFT/SET are frequently significant and effective, this may not apply to you in full, or to your particular problem. A lack of result or progress might mean that you need professional assistance. If you are already suffering from severe psychological problems, we highly recommend you seek professional advice and treatment.

Adverse reactions are extremely rare and, if any emotional intensity occurs during treatment, it is often the manifestation of a previous or underlying problem. Although EFT/SET may be of great help, if you believe you have long-standing or severe problems you should consider treatment with a qualified therapist.

If you experience any pain while using the techniques described in this book, stop immediately. Head or chest pain requires immediate medical advice, as do eye or vision problems, infections and dental problems, regardless of whether you feel better after using the Energy Techniques. Be aware that EFT/SET can mask or hide serious symptoms. Know what you are treating, if possible, and always use commonsense.

Finally, although research and clinical support are mounting, EFT/SET are not yet widely accepted as formally validated scientific techniques and thus must be considered experimental in nature with no guaranteed outcome for any individual.

# How to Use this Book

This book is divided into six chapters to make reading easier. Chapter 1 gives you an introduction into emotional freedom. Chapter 2 gives you the background on the new Energy Techniques and how they were developed. Chapters 3 and 4 introduce you to two user-friendly Energy Techniques and show you how to use them (Chapter 3 introduces you to EFT and Chapter 4 introduces you to SET). Chapters 5 and 6 show you how to apply these new techniques to treat various emotional problems or to make important life changes.

If you want to start using the Energy Techniques straight away, feel free to skip ahead. Although we have included the information on EFT first because this was the first of the techniques to be developed, SET is the easier to learn and use, so many readers will find it easier to skip forward to Chapter 4 and get started. Then if you want, you can go back to Chapter 2 to learn more about the background and development of these techniques, or head to Chapter 3 to learn how to use EFT. Chapters 5 and 6 provide general and specific applications of these techniques in areas of importance to you.

We will use the term EFT/SET together where what we are teaching applies to both techniques. Where we are speaking specifically of one technique, we will refer to that technique by name. We do this to indicate that you can use either or both techniques in the situation being discussed, or that the outcomes we are discussing are equally likely to be achieved using either technique, NOT to indicate that we are referring to a blended method. The main thing is to realise that you can use either or both of these techniques to gain significant relief from emotional stress, and to promote your emotional wellbeing.

For your convenience, a Frequently Asked Questions (FAQ) section is included as an appendix, where you will find the most common answers we give. For the more scientific-minded, we've also provided an appendix on research to date.

# Chapter 1

# What is Emotional Freedom?

The basic meaning of 'emotional freedom' is to have the power to be yourself and to live your life without being restricted by other forces. In the emotional sense, it means the capacity to enjoy your life without being dragged down by toxic or negative emotions.

The most common blocking emotion people experience is fear, which is holding many people back from living the life of their dreams. In this book you will learn some simple techniques that you can use to overcome fear and move forward on your positive life goals.

Another very common emotional block people experience is anger, usually fuelled by hurt feelings towards others and the way they treat us. When people 'do their thing' (i.e. do something hurtful or unjust) and you have to react in a certain way, by either getting upset or angry, then you are not emotionally free in that situation. However, if you are able to rechannel your emotional reactions and negotiate from a position of calmness and clarity, we would say that you are emotionally free in that situation.

Negative emotions are natural and normal; they are meant to arise, move through your system (and be processed), and ultimately leave you, hopefully making you wiser as a result. Often, however, they disrupt our system on their way through, even becoming 'stuck' somehow, and cause primitive and, sometimes, inappropriate reactions and outbursts.

Some negative emotions such as hurt, grief and feelings of loss and loneliness are inevitable in life. However, this is incompatible with simultaneously feeling cheerful, joyful or having feelings of wellbeing — *your natural state*. You are, in effect, bound by the negative emotions.

So freedom means being able to stay calm; to avoid being 'hooked' by fear or worry; to act thoughtfully even if you have feelings of doubt in a situation; to recover quickly from legitimate upset; and to be able to enjoy life, despite its challenging conditions.

It is because of the following two factors that you are not usually 'free':

- Negative emotions are quickly and automatically triggered, often by thoughts, through your body's primitive 'alarm system'.

- You have no way of reliably settling such feelings down.

One of our aims in this book is to teach you how to 'free yourself' by using Energy Techniques. Based on our observations and results after working with thousands of people both personally and professionally for over ten years, we have created some basic strategies for personal development using these cutting-edge, practical and effective Energy Techniques.

Perhaps the best test for any technique is whether the practitioner uses it regularly and confidently with their family and friends. We both have used, and continue to use, these techniques on a daily basis, and in this book we will give you powerful examples of how the techniques have benefited us and our loved ones. From relieving the night-time fears of young children, to overcoming severe life challenges like coping with the death of a family member, we have found a variety of applications for the techniques shown here, and we hope you are inspired to apply them in your own life as well.

Here is a real-life example from Charles, a participant in one of our workshops, who wrote about his experiences after several weeks of using these Energy Techniques:

*'I feel absolutely fantastic. Not just good or great, but more alive, content and at peace with myself than I can ever remember feeling. And it's not just because of the weather or because it's the weekend, but it's something much deeper and more profound and deep rooted than that ... It's hard to describe the shifts that have taken place. It's not just that my thoughts have turned relentlessly optimistic, or that every day I marvel at what a fantastic life I have, or that the world seems so filled with possibilities when only a few weeks ago it seemed full of limitations, frustration and anguish. It's like a heavy shroud of darkness has been lifted off me. I feel totally different in my body — bigger, stronger, lighter, more upright, full of potential and charged with energy flowing from top to bottom and bottom to top ...*

*I have done a lot of work on myself over the past twelve years, including yoga, homeopathy, therapy, meditation, affirmations, rebirthing, as well as reading dozens of self-help books. But nothing has created change so quickly and so effortlessly as EFT ... I look forward to my 30-minute tapping session each morning and am constantly amazed what memories and insights occur to me as I tap away ... the negative beliefs are rapidly transformed ... they lose all the power they had over me. Nothing much has changed in my outer world — I still have the same material concerns as before, but my attitude towards them has changed. I am so much more approving of myself, with all my foibles, and so much more positive in my outlook to life ... I feel like you have given me the most precious gift.'*

We hope this has piqued your interest in learning more about these powerful techniques. If so, let's begin ...

# Chapter 2

# The Energy Techniques

The 'revolution' of Energy Psychology refers to a new class of self-help and treatment tools, which can have impressive outcomes when treating common emotional conditions. If you have excess anxiety or fear (to name the two most responsive emotional states), the results of this treatment can be profound.

In this book, we'll describe two very effective Energy Psychology techniques called Emotional Freedom Techniques (EFT) and Simple Energy Techniques (SET) and will show you simple ways to apply them to achieve emotional relief. The basic component for each of these techniques is a simple process of lightly stimulating, usually by tapping, on specific energy points on the body using your fingertips. As you'll see, this simple process can frequently provide impressive results.

Without being professionally trained, you can potentially achieve very effective results in relieving emotional pain and hurt, especially with the stresses and difficulties of daily living. The 'inbuilt' relaxation and stress management tools of Energy Techniques make them a natural and effective alternative to drug remedies, including alcohol, cannabis and nicotine!

# What are EFT and SET?

Emotional Freedom Techniques (EFT) and Simple Energy Techniques (SET) are emotional healing tools from the field of Energy Psychology. These techniques, which we also refer to as Energy Techniques, represent a true combination of Eastern and Western medicine. Based on the theory that the cause of negative emotions may be attributed to a disruption in the body's energy system, EFT/SET can be thought of as the *psychological use of the acupuncture meridians.*

In fact, EFT/SET are often referred to as 'psychological acupressure — without the needles'. Instead, you relieve symptoms by tapping (or rubbing) various energy points on the body. This tapping is presumed to balance the energy meridians or channels on the body through which your energy flows — outlets that become disrupted when you think about or experience an emotionally disturbing circumstance. Once balanced, the upset is usually resolved — the memory typically stays but the emotional charge is gone and the result is usually lasting. Not only do you feel better afterwards, you are also able to think about the issue more clearly.

The basic premise behind these Energy Techniques is that negative emotions are caused by a 'disruption' in the body's energy system — they are not just held in the mind. After using Energy Techniques like EFT/SET, a damaging negative thought may no longer affect you, as if the associated feeling has been 'disconnected'. That thought will lose all power over your behaviour and in your beliefs. By intervening in the energy system to correct this disruption, EFT/SET can provide rapid relief from negative emotional problems, including phobias, trauma, hurt, anger, sadness, guilt, as well as many cases of physical pain. Both EFT/SET are really *body–energy techniques* that have profound psychological effects. While some other techniques may help change your thinking or behaviour, these Energy Techniques have the potential to change your life.

EFT/SET are part of a broader set of approaches which have been called variously Energy Psychology, Meridian Tapping Techniques, energy point stimulation, energy tapping, and more simply, Energy Techniques. We use the term Energy Techniques in this book because we find some of the other terms unwieldy and they also imply that you have to be a practitioner of traditional Chinese medicine, or a psychologist, to benefit. While many practitioners may incorporate these techniques with other therapies and techniques, we have found that the techniques alone can be used very safely and successfully for self-help, which is why we prefer the term Energy Techniques.

EFT and SET have many similarities, although there are also many differences, as you'll see. When using these approaches, you have the best of both worlds because if, for example, the simpler technique of SET isn't producing results, you can try adding some of the additional parts of EFT, and see if your results improve. And if EFT seems too complex, or you are finding it too hard to come up with the right words to target your problem, you can use the simple SET processes, and get excellent results. Many people are drawn to one technique, but it is likely that many people will use both of them at some point. We want you to know that you have that option available to you at all times. Remember, the best Energy Technique is the one that works for you.

# Why Use Energy Techniques?

EFT and SET are safe, gentle and natural techniques using your own body's energy system to help heal emotional distress. They each can positively influence the bodily symptoms of distress, pain and illness and generally balance functioning. These simple, yet powerful, techniques can be used for any difficult life situation.

There are four main benefits of using the Energy Techniques of EFT/SET:

- They are both very relaxing. Many people experience a relaxation effect within seconds of beginning either approach.

- They can desensitise and minimise negative or toxic emotions, and release 'stuck' emotions.

- The approaches can weaken the associated negative beliefs underlying your problems.

- After several weeks of practice the effect 'generalises' to your whole system and outlook, which becomes typically more light and optimistic.

Unless feelings of hurt and anxiety are dealt with, problems in relationships or life will never be resolved. EFT/SET can help you do this. When you're unhappy, change is scary, but not changing the cause of your unhappiness can be worse. This is where EFT/SET are exciting tools. They offer you a way to create change with the least amount of discomfort.

The Energy Techniques only 'work' on *negative emotions*. Positive and life-affirming emotions are not affected — we do not intend to eliminate legitimate sadness and difficulty in life, but are empowered to approach it with more courage and strength, using EFT/SET. Another way of thinking of this is that EFT/SET can help your negative emotions to move through you and cause you less discomfort as they do so. In our experience, both EFT/SET do this in the most gentle, life-affirming way.

You do not have to believe in EFT/SET in order for them to work. Our research and clinical experience has shown that many people, when introduced to these approaches, do not believe they will help them with their emotional difficulties. However, despite their disbelief, the vast majority of people have been able to use these simple techniques to achieve greater emotional freedom. Clearly, the changes produced owe more to the intervention in the body's energy system than to any beliefs that are present. So go ahead and try EFT/SET, despite any disbelief. You can be rest assured that this will not interfere with the results you achieve.

We expect first-time users to be sceptical, after all, these are very new techniques. However, it is our hope that you will not be cynical, or closed to the potential gain available to you with these techniques. We also don't expect you to believe without seeing results. In our experience, results will come to those who apply the methods, although some will need to use the techniques persistently in order to experience their full power.

Perhaps the most exciting thing about EFT/SET is that anyone can learn and use them for self-help purposes. While some more complex problems will require the intervention of a skilled therapist, ordinary people can learn EFT/SET and apply them to the many 'problems of living', often achieving a great deal of relief.

One of the most wonderful things about these techniques is that regular use of them will imbue you with a feeling of optimism and wellbeing, the likes of which you may not have experienced before.

# The Development of EFT/SET from TFT

About 30 years ago the Californian psychologist Dr Roger Callahan was studying the meridian system (the basis of acupressure and acupuncture) while he was treating a patient (Mary) with a severe water phobia. He had been unable to successfully treat Mary after 18 months of traditional therapy, but took note one day when she stated that the fearful feeling she was experiencing was located in her stomach. As there is a meridian point located directly under the eye which is linked to the stomach region, Callahan asked Mary to tap on that point, surmising that doing so might help to balance any disruption in energy which was occurring. Mary stated excitedly that the feeling was gone, and she happily proceeded to test this by rushing to the pool and splashing water over her face. Her lifelong phobia was gone, all from a few simple taps under her eye.

Following many other startling and amazing clinical results, Callahan developed a theory that tapping on the beginning or end points of 'involved' meridian channels, while attuning to a problem, will bring relief. He specifically hypothesised that when we think about, or experience, an emotional problem, we are tuning into a 'thought field'. Tuning into this 'thought field' activates 'perturbations' that can disrupt subtle energy flow. In theory, negative emotions result from these flow blockages, or perturbations. Tapping on the energy system releases these blocks, allowing energy to flow more freely. In addition, Callahan developed a theory of 'psychological reversal' where one is *paradoxically* motivated, that is acting contrary to our wishes and sabotaging ourselves. He instituted corrections in his treatment approach to deal with this and called it Thought Field Therapy (TFT).

Callahan had thus invented a comprehensive therapy for

psychological problems based on acupressure (stimulating acupuncture points manually) and kinesiology, using sequences of tapping points that produced extraordinary results in his clinical work over many years. And so began a new and exciting combination of using traditional Eastern medical practice with Western medical knowledge. In actual fact, Callahan's incredible discovery had its origin in ancient knowledge, which he was able to combine with other more recent findings about body systems and energy. The presence and flow of *energy* around and within the body has been extolled by ancient cultures, notably the Indian and Chinese, for thousands of years. The Hindus call it *prana* and the Chinese call it *qi*. While Western science has found no conclusive proof of the organisation of energy systems, the practice of bio-energy has been discovered to be vital to pain perception, healing and regeneration. Authorities regard it as belonging to the Universal energy field as well as to the organism; there is connection and flux.

Within the bio-energy paradigm, disease is seen as a 'disruption' of energy exchange and 'intoxication' of the body, especially through stress. A healer transmits the Universal energy through intention, words, the eyes and the hands to create order in the disturbed energy field of the sufferer. *Qi* energy creates order out of chaos in this way too. While this mystical explanation might perplex the scientist, the practical success of acupuncture, which uses the meridian system, has been demonstrated over many centuries. In the Chinese system of energy, there are twelve main meridians or circulation channels, while the Hindu system emphasises the seven energy centres called *chakras*. The bridge between the ancient knowledge of acupuncture meridian channels and the mind exists through Applied Kinesiology, which is the system of evaluating body functions with muscle testing and acupuncture points.

The American chiropractor Dr George Goodhart was the originator of kinesiology. In the 1960s he began to correlate body and mind functions holistically. Others followed, most notably Dr John Diamond, an Australian psychiatrist who developed a comprehensive approach to behavioural and emotional problems using kinesiology with his analytical and medical knowledge. He categorised the emotions conforming to each meridian channel, and therapeutic corrections for negative emotion.

These important discoveries preceded Callahan's pivotal experience with Mary, and contributed to the therapy he developed as a result.

## THE EVOLUTION OF EFT

Gary Craig (who trained with Callahan) experimented with a comprehensive set of energy points, which could be applied to treat any emotional problem. Rather than having to remember a large number of sequences of tapping points, or use complex diagnostic procedures, he developed one sequence that 'covers all the points' and called it Emotional Freedom Techniques (EFT). Craig found this approach to have an excellent success rate and has developed a number of improvements to enhance its results. In this book, we introduce you to this approach, as we originally learned it, and also outline for you the important improvements and refinements that have developed. We also introduce you to our own simplified approach, Simple Energy Techniques (SET), which grew out of our experiences and experimentation with EFT and other Energy Techniques.

## THE EVOLUTION OF SET

SET began as a simplified version of EFT and has become a stand-alone Energy Technique which emphasises the benefits of practical self-help through energy toning. It is now one of the most accessible Energy Techniques. As with EFT, SET primarily involves a simple process of tapping on the body's energy meridian points in order to relieve emotional stress.

SET developed out of our work with clients and our experiences with workshop participants. It also began out of our own attempts to follow the recommendations and model the processes used by Gary Craig, whose continual search to improve on Callahan's original discoveries has led to many innovative developments of huge benefit to the general public.

Gary encouraged us to continually stretch the boundaries and challenge the accepted wisdom and to continually seek improvements that would make these techniques even more accessible and useful to the average person. While we cannot hope to be in the same league as Gary Craig, and we continue to stand in awe of his achievements, we are thankful to be able to stand on the shoulders of this great innovator as we outline this approach and our findings, which we see as complementary to EFT. SET is outlined in full in Chapter 4.

Specific energy points are used for rebalancing or integrating in a variety of therapies, and the different techniques tend to share many common beliefs and practices. Many of these new Energy Techniques are extraordinary in their effectiveness, and generally produce shifts in toxic emotion and negative beliefs (see Appendix 3: Related Energy Techniques for a description of these).

The scientific validation of energy therapies has lagged behind such extraordinary results. However, recent research and others currently underway are rapidly changing this situation. Details of some of the more interesting studies that have been completed at the time of writing are included in Appendix 2: Research.

The extraordinary results of EFT/SET are unknown in pure acupuncture, or in Chinese medicine in a strict sense. Acupuncture for emotional issues often gives only general, mild relief. In contrast, there is something about holding the toxic problem in the mind while tapping on the energy points that causes the shift and change in a revolutionary way. This is not seen in either Western or Eastern medicine but is innate in the combination!

This is one of the things we like best about these new Energy Techniques — the fact that they represent a true East–West combination. At present, both Western and Eastern theories do not seem to fully explain what is happening, so we have come up with a new theory. As usual, the theoreticians are way behind the practitioners, who are forging ahead in learning new ways of helping people to gain greater emotional freedom.

We believe that in the future the role of the body's energy system in healing, and in being well, will be widely acknowledged and respected. It will lead to many new discoveries and paradigms, as the past decade has proved. Your study and application of these techniques forms part of this revolution.

## Choosing an Energy Technique

In this book we are presenting these simple and easy-to-learn methods for self-help purposes. Most likely you will notice results immediately, although not everyone will do so for every problem. We suggest you use one or both of the techniques, according to our directions, for at least one month. After that time you can judge for yourself how useful they are for you.

EFT/SET have been successfully applied to treat a wide range of emotional problems and issues, including anxiety, fears, phobias, trauma, post traumatic stress disorder (PTSD), grief, anger and guilt. They have also been applied to enhance performance and improve relationships.

Merely thinking and talking about emotional problems will usually not lead to permanent change, unless there is a corrective emotional experience sufficient to alter your beliefs. In some more modern therapies this could be quick; in more traditional therapies, such as psychoanalysis, this could be slow. No single technique or therapy offers complete healing, so it is wise to combine the best aspects of a range of models as much as possible. When the special attributes of energy healing are integrated with the tried-and-true traditional methods, we consider that you have the best of both worlds.

Many problems can be resolved very quickly when using EFT/SET. You should start to experience some shifts within the first few attempts, and very significant shifts can occur even after only one or two rounds of EFT (i.e. 3–5 minutes), or the equivalent time of continual tapping on the energy points as used in SET. More severe anxiety-based problems, however, may require anything from one to four sessions of a half-hour duration, or even longer for complete relief. Other problems may require persistence over a larger number of sessions, and you may need to persist with EFT/SET on a daily basis for 2–3 weeks. In the section on SET, we provide a way to do this which allows you to integrate the tapping into your daily life, and combine it with your regular activities. This persistence frequently results in complete relief, although results with addictions and depression are often harder to achieve and may require you to seek additional assistance from a trained professional.

The techniques used in EFT/SET make it possible to do a lot of good work in private, even if you are dealing with a deep fear. Usually your mind only has to make the fear appear a *little* for these Energy Techniques to provide some relief. For most people, just thinking about the problem will cause them to feel anxious; this is enough emotion to work on and it may not be necessary to go into the situation of greatest intensity in order to deal with it. In this way you can treat the problem very safely and effectively. You will find in the later sections on SET, that it is often possible to gain such relief just from stimulating the energy points on a daily basis, without even having to focus on them, or suffer the usual bad feelings.

Following either treatment, you will find that you can then go out into the real world and much of the emotional intensity of the usual fear reaction has gone! This has been our experience and that of thousands of people to whom we have taught these techniques.

Here's a great example of a practical and very personal application of this. David once wrote to Gary Craig, the creator of EFT, shortly after having his lifelong public speaking phobia treated in a single 38-minute treatment session at Gary's Ultimate Therapist Workshop back in February 1998. In his letter David wrote:

*'Dear Gary,*

*I would like to tell you exactly what I (and Steve Wells) have been up to this week in Melbourne and Sydney. Since the Ultimate Therapist Workshop, and my treatment with you, I had not volunteered for any public speaking. In truth, I didn't know if I was cured or not. My friend and energy brother Steve decided to "stretch" me and asked me to present a workshop about EFT with him; I said "yes" (moaning inside about what kind of a friend would test the therapy in such a direct way!). As the weeks passed towards* the date I found, to my alarm, that the first workshop had 40 therapists. Flying to the city involved a lot of tapping for a vague fear and a lot of "not knowing".

In the room, attendees began to arrive. Instead of feeling as if I was "walking the plank", I enjoyed meeting them ... still I believed that the problems would come when I was introduced, and when I actually had to do something. To my enormous (delighted) surprise NOTHING BAD HAPPENED! Even better, I was totally relaxed! My pulse didn't rise one extra beat ... my voice was firm ... breathing okay ... mind clear and responsive. What a feeling!

Well, I ran with this and had a great experience. Steve says he will tell the group too, but if I tell you that the first day involved leading a group through a pain minimisation procedure, and demonstrating my therapy with an individual session, and that the feedback was very good, then you can see I had to struggle mightily to avoid getting a swelled head! ... In fact, I would rate this day as one of the greatest experiences I have ever had — right up there with the birth of our first child.

So many people have now had benefit from the healing art of EFT and have been helped to learn and teach it too, all as a result of your professional and compassionate approach, Gary. Personally, I now think the sky's the limit, but we aren't going to take the credit for all this, are we? I am going to give the credit to you and Steve (and a bit to me — I did my best work!) but I think you would give it to God ...'

# Chapter 3

# Emotional Freedom Techniques (EFT)

Emotional Freedom Techniques (EFT) is the simple process of tapping on acupressure points on the body as you focus on your issue or problem. This tapping is presumed to balance the body's energy system and remove blockages in energy flow. Most people begin to notice positive results within minutes of first using EFT, and this deceptively simple process can often provide effective relief for emotional issues such as fears, phobias, anxiety, sadness, anger, grief or trauma. EFT is gentle, easy to learn and works. Once you learn it, you will have the power to relieve emotional stress.

To give you an idea of how EFT works, here's the EFT *short sequence* or *short version* steps, in order:

1. Start by rubbing a spot (sore spot) on the upper chest or tapping on the karate chop point on the side of the hand. This helps open up your energy system, and correct any energetic 'reversal'.

2. While you are doing this, make a set-up statement (initial phrase) about the problem.

3. Tap (using acupressure) on the seven specific energy points.

4. While you are doing this, focus on the problem, using the *reminder phrase*.

In this chapter, we explain these steps in detail and also include the *extended* version of EFT (thirteen energy points in total), because it is useful and shows the background of the technique in kinesiology. Although the long version helps if you are stuck, or want to treat problems more extensively, for most people in most situations, the short version will suffice.

In the beginning, concentrate on establishing the correct order and positions in the tapping sequence. When you have mastered the basics you can concentrate on the 'problem' more effectively. Later, you can use your intuition and vary the points if you wish.

## How to Use the Energy Points

Once you have identified a problem to focus on, you can commence EFT by rubbing the 'sore spot' on the upper chest. The sore spot is located by finding the hollow at the base of the throat with your finger. From there go straight down the breastbone about 7 cm and across to the left 90 degrees; at that place prod gently in a large circle until you find a spot that's sensitive or a little bit tender (see the diagram on page 26). It's a site of lymphatic congestion, hence the sensitivity. The technical term for this point is a 'neurolymphatic reflex point'.

If you have trouble locating the sore spot because it is not tender or sore for you, don't worry, it is located a little differently in some people. Either use the spot that is sensitive for you, or use the general area by rubbing in a large circle with the flat of your hand. You can also tap instead on the karate chop point (see page 35), if you wish.

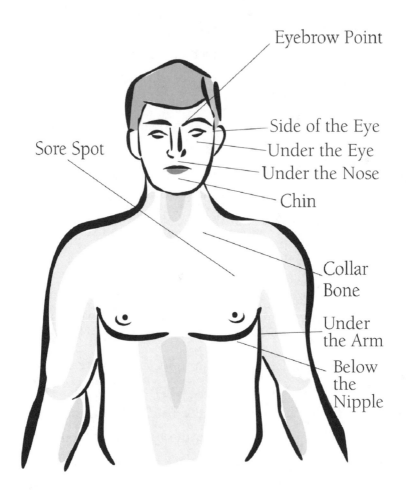

**Energy points in EFT**

There are a further seven tapping points in EFT that should be used in the following order:

1. The eyebrow point, which is more towards one eyebrow.

2. The side of the eye point, which is at the end of the eyebrow.

3. The under (the pupil of) the eye point in the centre of the cheek.

4. The under the nose point, in the midline.

5. The chin point, located under the mouth in the midline in the little indentation halfway between the lower lip and the chin.

6. The collarbone point, which is found by touching the hollow in the throat and feeling the two heads of the collarbones on either side; pick one head and tap directly underneath the collarbone. (Officially, this point is located at the junction where the sternum, collarbone and first rib meet.)

7. The under the arm point on the side of the body, approximately level with the nipple for men, or in the middle of the bra band for women.

There is an additional energy point directly below the nipple, which can also be used in the long version of EFT. For women this is located where the breast meets the chest wall. As this point can be difficult and embarrassing to access by some people, and there seems to be no problem with not using it, it is rarely used by most EFT practitioners. It is, however, included here for completeness for those who wish to tap on this point. It can be included in the sequence by adding it between the first seven points on the upper body and the hand points.

Once you have established where these points are on your body, you can start tapping. Using these points in this way stimulates the entire energy system via the meridian channels, according to Chinese theory.

To begin, use the first two fingers of your dominant hand. Tap 7–10 times on each point. (Do not be overly concerned with how many times you tap on each point — it is more important that you focus on your problem while tapping, rather than on counting the number of taps.) Make sure your tapping is light enough to feel, but not hard enough to hurt. This light touch will pay dividends. Either side of the body or face is good. Using either hand (or both) is also fine. Many people are concerned about tapping on only one side of their face or body and feel a need to balance this with tapping on the other side. However, since the meridian channels on both sides are identical this is not necessary. If you want to, that's fine, just realise that you do not *have to* tap on both sides in order to achieve results.

EFT is a very robust and forgiving technique. It will usually work for you, even if you vary the order and do not tap exactly on the points. Be precise at the beginning, and locate the points according to the diagram. Later, you will be able to get good results without being so exact. Landing close to the points is generally okay once you are familiar with the EFT sequence of tapping.

Points that 'attract' you, or which feel powerful, are points you can use more, and linger on, often for greater effect. Also, you may find that some points are a little tender or sore. This may mean that these points are good to tap on for longer, however, this must be balanced with the statement that a lighter tapping process may be helpful on these points — it isn't necessary to cause yourself pain for this method to work! If the process of tapping causes a lot of physical pain it is likely you are tapping too hard, so consider tapping more lightly, or tapping on the corresponding point on the other side of the body for a while.

It is helpful to take a deep breath in after each sequence of tapping finishes, as this helps your energy flow. Then reflect on how you feel about the problem for a moment and see how intense it makes you feel now. Continue with further rounds of tapping as long as you still have the intensity, or as long as you still have time! Realise that some problems may take a number of rounds of tapping and/or a number of sessions of tapping to achieve complete relief.

## Using the Right Words in EFT

EFT is not really a psychological technique, although it has huge psychological results in many people. It is more a body–energy technique, so it's not important to be clever, or to use a lot of words and psychological thinking when practising EFT. The best results come from doing the tapping when the negative feelings or reactions are strong, but it isn't necessary for those feelings to be overwhelming, of course. Just getting a slight hold of the negative feelings is enough to proceed. For many people, just thinking about the problem will be sufficient; for others, it may be necessary to focus on bodily feelings, or both.

In a focused EFT session it helps to be as specific as you can about the problem you want to resolve; if it is a negative feeling, for example, narrow it down to the part of the body where you might find it, and a specific emotional *intensity* (see page 40). Thoughts that cause distress often relate to a person, incident or time, as well as a specific fear.

## THE SET-UP STATEMENT

The set-up statement (or the initial statement) is always a variation on a basic theme. The 'set-up' is a way of using words to represent a problem — it actually acknowledges that you have a problem, whether it be a worry, a feeling, a fear, or any other emotion. It also represents the positive alternative, even if this seems not to 'fit' sometimes. You can have a problem and not be a bad person, or you can feel like a bad person, yet not own that belief completely either. There is room in our minds and in our words for both positive and negative parts of life to exist. In fact, this is an essential part of humanity — that we are multifaceted beings.

In constructing the set-up statement, you insert the words for the problem into a general statement, for example:

- 'Even though I have this fear of heights I accept myself.'

- 'Even though I have this bad problem, I'm a good person.'

- 'I accept myself deeply and completely even if I have this problem/feeling/difficulty/worry.'

We then suggest saying the statements out loud to reinforce the effect of the treatment, unless you feel it's more helpful to *imagine* what goes with the statement silently. You then proceed to say the set-up statement three times while you rub the sore spot.

When you say, 'I accept myself ...' it implies that you do *even if you might not believe this at the time*. When you say, 'I'm a wonderful person ...' there is also a part that will automatically check or respond that you're *not!* (according to any negative belief operating).

Whatever you say in the set-up statement as an affirmative phrase isn't the same as an ordinary affirmation. An ordinary affirmation is an exclusively positive statement, whereas a 'set-up' brings in the negative in your mind as well. Saying the negative, while you think or talk about the problem, *does not make the problem worse* in EFT! The energy point tapping will take care of the negative energy as part of the treatment. EFT works well on the negative, which is one of the main reasons why this technique is so safe — it allows you to work on issues that are 'black, white or shades of grey' and make progress.

You can even say, 'I accept myself *even though it's hard to accept myself*' or 'Even though I do not accept myself, *I deeply and completely accept myself!*'

## THE REMINDER PHRASE

The reminder phrase is a shorthand description of the problem you are targeting. You say the reminder phrase once while you tap on each of the spots. For example, it might be something like 'this stomach emotion' or 'this spider phobia' or 'this fear of heights' and it serves as a 'hook' to help the mind focus in on the problem while you tap.

A problem can have many parts or aspects. It is best to focus on a specific part and not on all of the problem at once. That way you will get a more marked relief of tension and the effect of EFT will not be diluted.

# The EFT Tapping Technique

In EFT, the tapping *itself* is as important as the thought or feeling that you use as a 'hook' in your statement to focus on the treatment. Make sure that you do a lot of tapping even if, in some instances, you aren't quite sure exactly what you are tapping on! In EFT, your subconscious mind knows what you need to treat. Activating the energy system is the important thing. Remember, tap on each point 7–10 times and make sure the tapping is light enough to feel, but not hard enough to hurt.

Some important hints to keep in mind when you start tapping are:

- If you tap near the meridian point you will still succeed, even if you aren't tapping exactly on the point itself.

- Tapping with two fingers instead of one is the best way to ensure you are tapping on or near the point.

- If you don't say the words correctly, your mind still knows what you intend. The important thing is to focus on the problem part you are working on, and follow what happens, like a discovery. Even thinking about doing it will begin the effect after a while.

The above statements about tapping also apply to SET (which is described in Chapter 4).

## THE EFT SHORT SEQUENCE

Earlier we introduced the EFT short sequence. Here we describe the steps in detail, so you can achieve the full benefits from this version of EFT.

The EFT shortcut sequence comprises two main parts:

1. The set-up and

2. The reminder phrase and seven energy points.

Perhaps the best way to explain how to use the short sequence of EFT is to give you an example. Let's say you have a fear of public speaking and the thought of getting up in front of an audience causes you to feel extremely anxious.

To begin, you must identify the anxious feeling and rate how intense it feels *right now while you are thinking about it*. We usually use a 0–10 rating, where 0 represents no intensity or bad feeling at all and 10 is the worst it could be. Let's say your rating is 9 out of 10.

You now need to construct the set-up statement, for example:

**'Even though I have this fear of public speaking, I fully and completely accept myself.'**

There are many alternative ways of wording this, and the statement will be different depending on what you are aware of when you think about your problem. Instead of 'this fear of public speaking' you might be aware of 'this tension in my stomach' and would focus on this instead.

You then repeat this statement three times while rubbing on the sore spot or tapping on the karate chop point (see page 35). Then you tap, in turn, on each of the seven points while remaining tuned into or focused on your fear.

At this point it can also help to repeat a reminder phrase, such as 'this public speaking fear' as you tap on each point. Its purpose is to keep your mind and body tuned into the problem. You would then start the tapping process by tapping 7–10 times on the eyebrow point, then proceeding through the sequence as follows: side of the eye, under the eye, under the nose, chin, collarbone and under the arm. At each point be sure to stay focused on your problem and/or repeat the reminder phrase. If you have a strong image or feeling it is not essential to repeat the reminder phrase as long as you keep your attention on the distressing feelings and/or images while you go through the tapping routine.

When you have tapped on each of the seven points, take a deep breath in and check your fear feeling to see if it has changed.

The next step is to proceed through the various aspects of the problem until nothing about the issue causes you any distress. Often, this just means continuing to tap on the fear feeling until it subsides completely. However, it can also mean identifying related feelings, identifying events from our past that relate to the problem, identifying bodily sensations, and identifying underlying beliefs that need to be treated. Sometimes your problem will not be completely relieved until these associated aspects and beliefs are addressed. More detail on how to proceed through these is provided later in the book. For now, simply realise that whatever comes up in your mind and body that is related to the problem is what is worth tapping on.

## THE EXTENDED EFT SEQUENCE

The extended EFT sequence was the original basic recipe for EFT as outlined by Gary Craig before he discovered that a shortcut sequence was often all that was required for effective treatment. Many EFT practitioners routinely use the shortcut version and only add the additional steps in the longer version if they are not getting progress. We recommend you use a similar process.

The extended version of EFT has four main parts:

1. The set-up.

2. A sequence of tapping on the twelve energy points — the basic seven plus the five hand points.

3. The nine-gamut sequence.

4. A second sequence of tapping on the twelve energy points.

The extended version of EFT uses the seven points we have already outlined for the short version and also incorporates several points on the hand. These are:

- The thumb nail point, which is located on the side of the thumb where the nail joins the flesh in the corner, on the palm side of the thumb.

- The finger points on the index, middle and little fingers, which are the same corner location at the fingernail, on the thumb side.

- The karate chop point, which is a little higher than halfway up the middle of the chop strike area on the side of the hand between the wrist and little finger.

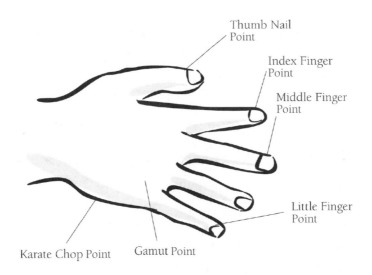

Thumb Nail Point

Index Finger Point

Middle Finger Point

Little Finger Point

Karate Chop Point       Gamut Point

**The finger points used in EFT**

## THE NINE-GAMUT SEQUENCE

In addition to the energy points used, there is a group of nine activities that you perform while continuously tapping on the *gamut point* on the back of the hand. This point is located in the groove between the two end knuckles (i.e. back from the little finger and ring finger) on the back of the hand when you make a fist, about 1 cm back towards the wrist. The nine-gamut sequence is believed to assist the organisation of the brain by alternately stimulating the left and right hemispheres, hence the strange nature of the 'tasks' in the sequence.

The nine actions involved are:

1. close your eyes

2. open your eyes

3. eyes hard down right (keeping your head still)

4. eyes hard down left (keeping your head still)

5. roll your eyes in a circle either clockwise or anti-clockwise

6. roll your eyes in a circle the other way

7. hum a short tune for 5 seconds (e.g. 'Happy Birthday')

8. count out loud to five

9. hum a short tune again for 5 seconds.

### Putting the Extended Sequence Together

Now you can start using the extended version of EFT. Begin by identifying a problem to work on. Let's say, as above, it is a fear of public speaking. As with the short sequence, start by identifying the feeling associated with your problem and rate how intense it feels *right now*. Use the 0–10 rating, where 0 is no intensity or bad feeling at all and 10 is the worst it could be. Again, let's say your rating is a 9.

Next construct your set-up statement in the same fashion as you did for the short sequence:

**'Even though I have this fear of public speaking, I fully and completely accept myself.'**

Repeat the set-up statement three times while rubbing on the sore spot or tapping on the karate chop point (see page 35), then tap in turn on each of the twelve energy points while remaining tuned into or focused on your fear: the eyebrow, side of the eye, under the eye, under the nose, chin, collarbone, under the arm, thumb, index finger, middle finger, little finger and karate chop. Again, you can repeat a reminder phrase such as 'this public speaking fear' as you tap on each point, if you feel it helps. As mentioned before, if you have a strong image or feeling it is not essential to repeat the reminder phrase, as long as you keep your attention on the distressing feelings and/or images while you go through the tapping routine.

Now complete the nine-gamut sequence. While tapping continuously on the gamut spot you proceed through the nine actions: eyes closed, eyes open, eyes down right (keeping your head up while doing these actions), eyes down left, roll eyes clockwise, roll eyes anti-clockwise, hum a short tune, count to five, and hum a short tune. Remember to keep tapping on the gamut point while doing the actions.

Once you have completed the nine-gamut sequence, complete another round of tapping on each of the twelve energy points as before while remaining tuned into your fear.

When you have finished tapping on the points, take a deep breath in and check your fear feeling to see if it has changed.

If you have some remaining emotional intensity on the issue, do another round on the 'remaining feeling' and continue to do this until the intensity is reduced to a zero. If you become aware of other problems and feelings as you go, carry out additional rounds of tapping while focusing on this new or related problem, until each is cleared. Clear out as much of your emotional baggage as you can and accept nothing less than total freedom.

## What Do You Do When You Have Completed a Round of EFT?

When you have gone through the entire tapping sequence once, we term this a 'round'. When you have completed a round of EFT you should check in and see how you are feeling on the problem you have targeted. It is helpful to rate the emotional intensity at this point.

When you commence a second or third sequence for a particular problem, adjust the words in the set-up statement to reflect the fact that you are targeting the 'remaining problem'. For example, if you have been treating a fear of spiders, during the first round you may focus on 'this spider fear'. On subsequent rounds of the technique where you treat this fear, adjust the phrasing to refer to the 'remaining spider fear'. Do this even if the intensity did not seem to reduce significantly in the first round. Alternatively, you may need to adjust the set-up statement and reminder phrase to reflect other parts of the problem, or even related problems. See the discussion on aspects on page 44 for a description of how to do this.

We have found in our years of working with EFT that if you *emphasise the negative aspects* of a problem *while tapping repeatedly*, the results are far better than trying to think that all will be well. This is strange but true. While you may have learned that it is best to think positively, this often does nothing to treat the problem you are focusing on, other than to distract your attention. In EFT (and also with SET) it is important to focus on the negative problem in order to 'tune into' it for the treatment to work. Surprisingly, when you do this, instead of the negative feeling that normally accompanies the problem prevailing, the tapping process assists the negative feelings to shift, and they are usually replaced by more positive feelings and thoughts.

After the EFT treatment, your affirming positive thoughts and wishes will be far more likely to bear fruit, as they are no longer blocked. Many people find that the results of specific work are very rapid indeed, however, for some problems you may need to give time and space to this practice over several weeks in order to see the full benefits of the treatment. It is often possible, with EFT, to quickly overcome problems that have resisted the usual 'positive thinking' advice for years.

## How Often Should You Practise?

The answer to this question is really *as much as you want* to get better! Integrate EFT into your daily routine — say 6–10 times a day — or set aside time several times a week for a session of 15–20 minutes of tapping. In between times you can make a note of problems that occur to you for these sessions.

## Don't Just Feel the Fear — Treat it!

There is a popular idea that when approaching something you fear, such as public speaking, you should simply feel the fear and go ahead anyway. In EFT we say there is no need to put yourself through such an ordeal. In fact, in using EFT, while we need to 'tune into' or 'focus on' the fear when we are treating it, it is not really necessary to get into the strongest part of the emotion. Usually just thinking about it is enough.

When you have treated your fear it is tempting to want to brave it out and go ahead to confront the object of your fear even though you still have some low levels of intensity. We believe it is usually better to continue your EFT work until there is minimal or (preferably) no intensity at all on the issue, and then move forward.

When you have freedom on the issue of fear, then your decisions are made voluntarily from a position of calm. Many people do not believe this is really possible to achieve, however, we have personally experienced such an outcome, and so have thousands of people worldwide after using EFT (and SET). It is a common belief, for example, that anxiety is necessary for good performance. Not so. More often anxiety gets in the way of peak performance, distracting your attention and focus. There is a difference between excitement and anxiety which no amount of positive thinking or reframing will help you to realise. Treating your fear with Energy Techniques like EFT and SET, however, can help you to free your energy and attention so that your focus is entirely on the performance, and not on the fear.

## How Can You Measure Your Progress?

So, how do you know the intensity of a problem is diminishing and the treatment is working? It is simply the way you feel about the problem when you focus on it. The intensity relates to an emotional level — not the way you think — and guides you in your feeling. When you 'rate' the intensity of your problem with a number out of 10 (where 0 is no intensity, and 10 is the worst feeling you can imagine), it represents the level of distress that the problem gives you now.

It is essential to separate the thought from the feeling when you are trying to find out the result of EFT. After treatment we often ask people:

'When you think, now, about what was bothering you, how much does it upset you, or stir you up? Not the thought of it, which might not have changed, but how much feeling-reaction do you have?'

There is often a surprising difference, in that the emotional 'heat' of the problem is now much less.

When EFT works well, you may find that the intensity drops while you tap on the points, and that you can't find the same level of distress afterwards! This is normal for the technique. You should experience this lowering of intensity for most common everyday anxieties.

It also doesn't mean that if the intensity of a problem has a low number (i.e. it's not distressing to you), that you can't work on the problem. It just means that you feel only a little of it at present. That's good — we don't want dramas, just a mental 'hook' for you to hang the problem on while you work with the tapping.

If you think of several aspects of a fear, choose to use EFT first with the most intense one — you're likely get a better result overall. Likewise with particular painful incidents or hurts — choose the strong parts of them to work on first.

During self-treatment, aim to reduce most intensities to a very 'low number' (such as 2, 1 or 0), particularly the body sensations of tension, such as a pounding heart, 'butterflies' in the stomach or throat constriction.

It is possible that you can still bring up distressing images or thoughts after you have been tapping on a problem. What is important is to identify how much intensity these thoughts or images produce in you when they arise — not what you think they will bring up in the future, but how much intensity they produce *now*? It can be a mistake to assume that your problem is no different simply because you can still come up with these images. The images themselves are not important — what is important is how much intensity they produce in you when you think of them. Many of our clients have been convinced that their problem remains simply because *in their mind* they can still see themselves getting upset, yet their problem is actually resolved because the images of that situation no longer upset them. They are often surprised to find that when they confront the previously distressing situation, no intensity occurs whatsoever.

## The Generalising Effect

The generalising effect is a wonderful bonus of these Energy Techniques, and applies to both EFT/SET. What this means is that if you apply EFT/SET to several large issues and you treat these completely, or if you use the technique persistently over a period of time (e.g. for a few weeks), the effects can generalise to your other emotional issues. For example, if you have suffered a large number of traumatic experiences and you apply EFT/SET in turn to several of the most intense of these then, usually, the other associated experiences will not feel as intense when you think of them either, despite the fact that you have not applied the technique to them directly. This is so refreshing to realise, particularly for people who think that with the large number of bad experiences in their past, they will require significant time and effort in order to get relief. Typically this is not so at all — the work you have done in the early stages really begins to pay off and the effect spreads to other areas of your life.

When you practise regularly over several weeks, a wonderful feeling of lightness and optimism often occurs. If you practise the relaxing techniques of EFT/SET and get a 'shift' when using them on negative emotions, then you can expect this generalising effect later. It also makes a host of minor life problems far more trivial for you; suddenly you realise you are cruising along without any excess anxiety or worry! This is a great tonic.

## Making Sure Your Healing is Complete

EFT is a very simple technique to learn; so simple, in fact, that many people don't realise just how much it can do for them if they continue to apply it. It is highly rewarding and effective in eliminating a lifelong phobia or a long-standing trauma or hurt. However profound this may seem, there is no need to stop there. Several former clients have contacted us in the past, some time after treatment, asking to see us again for more treatment on a new problem. We typically ask them if they have considered using EFT (or SET) for that problem. Often their reaction is, 'Oh yes, I suppose I could!' and they go away and try the approach on this new problem, often finding that this is sufficient. Some, of course, have more difficult issues that require the concentrated attention that a therapy session provides and often need the combined effect of several methods. The important thing is to give the techniques a try — you have nothing to lose by doing so! We recommend you go as far as you can go with these techniques. Regardless of the path that you must inevitably take, we say total freedom should be your ultimate aim. Many people will be surprised to learn just how easy this seemingly elusive state can be achieved with sufficient application of these Energy Techniques.

Remember, it is important to test the result; it is important to seek out any possible thing that can provoke some intensity for you and treat it; it is important to persist; and it is important to keep using the technique on other issues and problems.

As Gary Craig recommends: try it on everything! And be persistent …

Once you have achieved some results with your own issues with EFT, be sure to share your good fortune around! However, prior to doing this we recommend doing some rounds of EFT on yourself for your anxiety about other people changing — sometimes if you present them with EFT out of your desire for them to change, it can get in the way of them achieving good results with the technique.

## Dealing with Aspects

Your emotional problems can often have many aspects, or parts, and it may be necessary to treat each of these in order to gain complete relief on the issue you are treating. The solution is to persist in applying EFT to the various aspects, but you have to understand what we mean by 'aspects'. (This discussion on aspects also applies to the SET technique, so we will refer to them both here. Once you have learnt SET, you may wish to come back to these pages.)

## FEELINGS

Aspects may be a set of related feelings. For example, you may feel fearful about a situation, yet at the same time feel embarrassed and angry with yourself for having these feelings. These related feelings are other aspects of the problem. It is likely that each of these feelings will need to be treated in order for you to experience complete relief. This is not usually difficult. The process simply involves identifying every negative feeling that you have related to the problem and applying the EFT/SET process to these. This is being aware, without having to be a psychologist or to label every feeling with a word.

## EVENTS

Aspects may be a set of *related events*. For example, you may have had several experiences that relate to the problem you are treating. Let's say, for example, that you have a fear of public speaking. It's possible that you have several memories of different situations in school and perhaps somewhere later in life where you had a bad experience performing in front of a group of people. You may need to go over each of these experiences and apply the EFT/SET procedure to it — and to the related feelings — in order to experience complete relief from this issue. And, remember, if you have a large number of these, treating a few of them well will usually mean that the effect generalises to the others.

## THOUGHTS OR BELIEFS

Aspects may be a set of related thoughts or beliefs. We will treat the issue of beliefs separately, because often there are underlying beliefs, and these may be subconscious, which means we are not always aware of them, and they may be blocking the problem. Some of these beliefs may also be very conscious. Just ask yourself: 'What do I think about this problem and my ability to get over it?' Once you have identified any negative or limiting beliefs you can then simply apply EFT/SET to the belief by repeating the belief statement as you apply the tapping procedure.

## BODILY SENSATIONS

Aspects may be a series of bodily sensations. Sometimes when we start applying EFT/SET to bodily sensations we end up experiencing other bodily sensations. The process to follow here is what Gary Craig calls 'chasing the pain'. Simply continue to apply EFT to whatever bodily sensations arise until you experience relief.

## A COMBINATION OF ASPECTS

Aspects may be a combination of all of the above. An example may be found in a client that Steve worked with who had a fear of going to the beach due to a strong phobia of sharks. A short way into the EFT process, as we were tapping on 'shark fear', she experienced pain in her right knee. We then proceeded to apply EFT to her 'right knee pain'. During this process, she suddenly started to visualise snakes and lizards, which she was also fearful of. We proceeded to apply EFT to her 'snakes and lizards fear' and the knee pain returned. We then applied EFT to the knee pain, which then reduced. After this short session, the client was able to visit the beach without fear and also had eliminated her related phobia of snakes and lizards.

So the message with aspects is to **follow whatever comes up** and **persist with the EFT/SET process**.

If you are tapping on a particular problem or issue, what if the level of intensity goes up? This implies that your mind has shifted to a different *aspect* of the problem and you should begin afresh in that case and treat it as a 'new' part of the problem. It's wise to follow the thoughts and feelings that might be linked to those changes.

Sometimes it can happen that we 'tap into' an emotion or situation that is more intense than the one we started with. If this happens to you, continue the tapping procedure on this new emotion and persist until it reduces. Finding an underlying problem such as this is a good thing, as it gives you an opportunity to relieve a great deal of your ongoing pain and suffering.

You can't predict how much EFT treatment a particular problem requires. Sometimes results are amazingly quick; sometimes they are not. Commonsense tells us that a complex problem will have many aspects, and will take a lot of persistent tapping work. A 'simple' fear or phobia might need only a short period of treatment.

Clinical experience with difficult problems — those with hundreds of aspects — indicates that when you treat around a dozen aspects comprehensively with EFT (which ultimately may take a few hours of tapping), the remaining ones do not generally bother you emotionally any more. If they do still bother you, this usually means you have more tapping to do, but it may also mean you need to consider professional assistance.

Think 'around' the problem — go wherever your *reactions and associations* take you and follow these. Some examples of questions that may help you think around the issue are:

- Are there people connected to the issues?
- What about the first/worst/last time you felt the feeling?
- What specifically upsets you the most?
- What does your intuition tell you about the connections to this problem?

Remember to be thoughtful and persistent.

## Example of an EFT fear reaction treatment

*Fear of Flying*

This is an account of a treatment session using EFT with a woman who had a fear of flying. It will be very instructive for you to read, as it will give you plenty of ideas for addressing aspects when working on your own fears or emotional issues.

This lady (we will call her 'Anne') was able to fly but felt 'sick and scared'. The problem had begun twelve months ago following a stormy flight.

We started by identifying the physical reaction accompanying the fear — the thought of flying. Anne was aware of her *pounding heart*, and rated this as a '9' on the 0–10 scale (remember: 0 = no intensity at all; 10 = the worst it could feel). We treated this with three rounds of EFT until the feeling was at a very low intensity. (Although I say 'we' treated this, remember that Anne is doing the tapping on herself, just as you will be on your own emotional issues.)

We then applied EFT to the *remaining* feeling. After two more sequences, the resulting intensity was at a level 2. Anne reported that her body felt calm.

We then moved to imagining the *worst* flight possible, and completed two EFT sequences (again, the resulting intensity was a '2'), then we followed this up by *exaggerating* the flight a little (two EFT sequences, resulting in an intensity of '3'). This technique of exaggerating the bad can actually be very helpful in focusing your mind on the most intense part of the fear. Then you can treat it.

We then looked at a *recent* fear episode aspect. After two EFT sequences the resulting intensity was a '1'.

We then searched for any specific aspects that provoked fear and tapped on the thought of the *plane 'dropping'*. After three sequences on this aspect, Anne's intensity had dropped to zero.

We then moved to testing the fear, that is, imagining the situation in the *future*. This is very important to do and, in Anne's case, provoked some intensity, which two sequences reduced to an intensity of '1'.

The next stage involved *checking* the fear (or 'sick feeling') in the body. After one EFT sequence, the resulting intensity was zero.

We then went on to check the issue of *safety* and had Anne complete one EFT sequence on the thought that 'I won't be safe if I get over this fear'.

We then checked the *deserving* issue and had Anne make the statement: 'I don't deserve to get over this fear of flying' as she completed one EFT sequence.

We then treated her *anger at herself* for 'having the problem for so long, and not handling it better'. Two sequences were done on this as Anne could identify some anger here.

We finished with a *general check* and Anne could identify no intensity at all on any present or future aspect. Her body was completely calm. She had no remaining symptoms.

Anne was advised to *practise EFT* at home for one week, and prior to or during a flight, if necessary. This is essential to maintain calm and to deal with the *fear of the unknown* — that is, not being able to believe in the cure until dealing with the real event.

Overall, the total number of EFT sequences was 21 and the total time taken for the treatment was 45 minutes. The result was that Anne was able to have a successful flight with no fear at all, but with a lot of surprise and satisfaction. This is the sort of result you should expect on issues that provoke fear and anxiety, while realising that different problems may require different levels of persistence owing to the different aspects and associated beliefs.

An important thing to note in the treatment above is that it would be tempting to finish the treatment when you have achieved a zero or a level 1 of intensity on any aspect of the fear. Many of our clients would have been very happy to stop the treatment at an even higher level until we let them know that they really could do better. If you are used to the fear being at a level 9 or 10, then having it move to a level 5 seems like a miracle. It can seem hard to believe that the results can actually be even better than this.

The other thing to note is the importance of checking the results and looking everywhere possible to locate additional aspects related to the problem. We want to be sure to get it all. If your doctor were operating on a tumour, you would want to be sure that the removal was complete. It is every bit as important to identify all the aspects of a problem that are bothering you and remove the intensity from all of them. And you don't want to get into the situation and find that something you haven't thought of has arisen to upset you.

## Additional Tapping Locations

There are some additional points that can be added to the EFT sequence (and they may also be used in SET). These include the top of the head, as well as the wrist points. These points were introduced to us by Dr Michael Gandy, and have become a staple component of most EFT treatment.

The *top of the head* point is located at the crown right on top of the head (see diagram on page 66). It can be tapped using all the fingers of one hand. Many people like to tap around the top of the head in a small circle using all the fingers of one hand (or both hands if you prefer).

There are also two wrist points, one on the inside wrist, and the other on the outside wrist, in a corresponding position. Each is located about 2–2.5 centimetres from the main wrist crease, where the wrist and hand join (see diagram on page 67).

It is common to tap on the wrist points using the flat of the hand, which means you don't have to worry about locating the point precisely. Another way of tapping on the inner wrist point is to tap the wrists of both hands together.

The top of head and wrist points can be added to the EFT sequence at any point, however, they are typically included either at the beginning or at the end of the regular tapping sequence, whether using the long or short version of EFT.

Many EFT practitioners also add the top of head point to the seven-point sequence, as this is a combination point in traditional Chinese medicine, meaning it is considered the meeting point of a number of energy meridians, and is potentially quite powerful in its effects. The fact that this point is also one of the points in the chakra system of energy centres may mean it is an especially powerful point.

EFT will typically work for you whether or not you include these additional points, and many people have achieved excellent results using just the seven-point shortcut sequence mentioned earlier.

## Overcoming Blocks

If you become stuck when using EFT, the following ideas will usually help:

- Use the extended EFT sequence.

- Shift your focus between the body (sensations/feelings) and the mind (thoughts/ideas/images).

Ask yourself: 'What feeling goes with my thought? If I had to name a place in the body where it sits, where would it be?' (Tap on the points while focusing on the location and nature of that feeling).

Alternatively, if you have been 'following' some feeling in your body that is related to a problem, you could ask yourself: 'What thought goes with my feeling?' (Tap while focusing on that thought). Be spontaneous and blurt out whatever you think.

## DEALING WITH BLOCKING BELIEFS: PSYCHOLOGICAL REVERSAL (PR)

In EFT theory, psychological reversal (PR) is the term given to subconscious negative beliefs that hold you back from getting completely over a problem. We have all experienced some issues that we just can't seem to get over, no matter how hard we try. Also, at times it may seem that we sabotage ourselves, or 'shoot ourselves in the foot'. The culprit in most cases is the presence of one or more blocking beliefs, otherwise known as psychological reversal.

When PR is present, the energy of the body is said to be in an 'opposite' state and therefore not a healing energy. Gary Craig often describes this as like 'having your batteries in the wrong way'. When you turn the batteries around the right way, the energy flows normally. Callahan theorised that when PR is present our energy system is literally flowing in the opposite direction from the change that we desire to make. PR is hypothesised to be present in about 40 per cent of problems you attempt to treat with EFT. This means that if you don't correct it, you will not make the progress you desire.

The good news is that the EFT correction for PR is really very simple — as long as you are able to identify the underlying belief that is preventing you from moving forward. If you are worried about not being able to identify the specific negative beliefs that may be blocking your progress, then therapists using these techniques have identified some beliefs that are almost universally present. We provide a list of these on page 54. If you are not making progress it will be useful for you to consult this list and try the correction process using the belief statements we have listed. For many problems, this will enable you to get success with EFT where you previously could not.

Most PR can be corrected for a period of time by massaging the 'sore spot' while repeating a set-up statement. The karate chop point can also be used if the sore spot gets tender with a lot of use.

Theoretically, EFT treatment will not work smoothly in 40 per cent of sequences if the PR remains 'as is'. This is the reason why we do the set-up statement with the rubbing of the sore spot before each EFT sequence. It only takes a moment and will help clear a reversal if it is present.

Of course, since PR is present only about 40 per cent of the time, it is possible for you to go straight into the tapping sequence without doing the set-up statement and see if you get results. If not, return to doing the set-up process. You will also find further ways of shortcutting the process as you go along, and we will outline several of these later in the book.

Often the blocks to progress in treatment result from unexpected reversals. This condition is very common in addictions and depression.

If you are not making any progress when applying EFT to your problem, it may be because of a belief challenge.

## DEEPER NEGATIVE BELIEFS

You may be striking some deeper negative beliefs with PR, which may block your progress when using EFT to resolve any fears or problems. If this is happening, then say: 'I deeply and profoundly accept myself with all my faults and problems' while rubbing the sore spot. Now continue with your self-help.

Pay attention to the set-up statement for the problem, and bring in any negative beliefs, all the while tapping on any that are meaningful to you (using a sequence of EFT for each). For example:

'I don't believe I can get over this problem.'

'I don't deserve to get over this problem.'

'It's not safe for me to get over this problem.'

'Other people need me to have this problem.'

'I'll be a different person if I get over this problem.'

'It's too hard for me, I can't really get over this problem.'

'EFT is too weird to help me get over this problem.'

'I can't get over this problem myself.'

'I'm worried this problem might come back in the real world.'

'I can't/won't look after myself.'

'I can't practise — I'm not worth it.'

Remember, EFT works on the negatives and you need to tune into these while tapping in order to treat them. This also applies to negative beliefs. Even though it may feel like you are reinforcing the negative belief by stating it or focusing on it, if you are tapping on the energy points at the same time as focusing on the belief, you are more likely to lessen the emotional hold you have on that belief.

These are examples of personal blocks, and you probably have more of your own; they prevent you from becoming free of the reaction or behaviour in question.

## OTHER COMMON BLOCKS

There are some other common blocks, with each requiring a set-up statement and a sequence of tapping if you feel they are relevant to your problem. For example:

'I accept myself deeply and completely even if':

'I have too many problems.'

'I haven't got what it takes to get over this problem.'

'I can never get over this problem.'

'I won't allow myself to get over this problem.'

'This problem is part of me.'

'I'm afraid to get over this problem.'

'This problem is just too hard for me to get over.'

'I don't believe I can get over this problem.'

'I can't get over this problem completely.'

Remember, while thinking of the block that fits in your situation, use the block phrase as your reminder phrase.

## TYPES OF BLOCKING BELIEFS

Clinical psychologist Fred Gallo has identified several different types of reversal, all of which relate to underlying beliefs. The main ones are:

- Psychological Reversal (regular), which is treated by tapping on the karate chop point or rubbing on the sore spot while making a self-acceptance statement three times.

- Mini Psychological Reversal, which is the term used to describe a situation where you get only so far with a problem and no further. For example, you may get the emotional intensity down to a level 5, but be unable to get any further. To treat this, tap on the karate chop point or rub the sore spot and repeat the following statement three times prior to doing the tapping: 'I deeply and completely accept myself even though I still have some of this problem.'

- Massive Psychological Reversal, which is treated by rubbing on the sore spot with this self-acceptance statement said three times: 'I deeply and completely accept myself with all my problems and limitations.'

- Deep Level Psychological Reversal, which is treated by tapping under the nose with this self-acceptance statement said three times: 'I deeply and completely accept myself even if I never get over this problem.'

(For more information, see Fred Gallo's books, *Energy Psychology* and *Energy Tapping*.)

It is important to remember the following when facing any blocks:

- Do EFT on feeling 'angry with (yourself) for having the problem in the first place, and not handling it better!'

- Do at least two whole 'long' sequences while you ponder any anger/criticism/blame/judgement/ finding fault with yourself, and see if you feel different.

- You may be suffering from depression. Depression is a complex condition that can interfere with any progress, although EFT is good in helping mild to moderate depression.

Very often depression is hidden and EFT alone is not usually the main treatment.

- If you feel low, have poor concentration, feel physically sluggish, suffer from low self-esteem or feel that life is flat and no fun, go and see your doctor for a check-up.

- Energy work sometimes flows better in a different place. Move from room to room and see if this makes a difference. Drink a glass of water. You may also need to wait for a day, if you are having an allergic episode.

- Sometimes the effect of EFT takes place in a delayed fashion, after several hours, or even after several days.

- The key to success in many cases is persistence. This means a program of regular 'tapping' on all the aspects, even if this seems a little boring to the mind. It's like putting money in a savings account.

If you have tried our suggestions — and have been *very persistent* in practising — and nothing is working, consider contacting us or a therapist (especially one trained in Energy Techniques) for extra advice.

# The Apex Effect

The Apex Effect is a peculiar outcome that occurs for some people when using EFT/SET, where they may get over their problem but then not see EFT/SET as having anything to do with the resolution. Typically, this means that unless the energy treatment and results fit into your view of the world, you might think that the results have nothing to do with the tapping. Your mind will then come up with some idea to explain what has happened, since the treatment seems so strange.

One of the challenges with EFT/SET is that when they work quickly, the mind finds the result irritating sometimes, especially if you have wished for years to be free emotionally. It is difficult to grasp that a resistant phobia can suddenly no longer affect you. This is not due to 'distraction' or to 'suggestion' or to 'talking' about the problem, but it might seem that way. Therapists have been using such strategies for years without the additional extraordinary results possible with EFT/SET. It can take time to 'adjust' to not having the problem as it used to be.

## Getting Help When You Need It

It is possible that self-help may not suit you. Self-help may not be enough because of the need to be heard and understood (it's lonely being your own therapist!). You may have come to the realisation that you have problems that are not minor. Going further means looking for a one-on-one session with a therapist or visiting your GP for a physical check-up. Sometimes a physical condition can cause mental and emotional problems, as can medication, so this needs to be ruled out.

If you are not clinically depressed, which means you have depressing problems without having the disorder of depression, then you will probably need to see a psychologist or a psychiatrist or a counsellor.

If you do have depression, then it's wise to accept treatment, which can include both traditional and alternative methods, because depression is a complex condition that takes away self-confidence, strength and concentration.

Having therapy means finding another person whom you trust to listen to you and help you find out what's important and real for you.

As a healing tool EFT promises much, and regularly delivers. It is a great relaxation and stress-management technique, and can do so much more.

If EFT is used in a thoughtful way, you might be surprised to find that typical reactions of fear, anger and sadness are minimised in your daily life. In other words, after regular practice of EFT, you might not react to the irritating and frustrating 'grind' as you once did.

For anxieties and fears EFT can be used very specifically to bring relief and hope. All of the useful and helpful ideas and thoughts you have tried to use before to help yourself, but couldn't because you were 'locked in' to negativity, can now bear fruit.

No method can work for everyone or in every situation. We have discussed 'blocks' and difficulties caused by strong negative belief systems, but if you have been successful before and come across a problem that won't 'move', consider having a professional assessment, ideally from someone trained in these methods.

EFT is part of a new approach to living and coping. Although many discoveries are being made in the field of energy work, EFT is here now in practical form. It works. Use it in good health.

# Chapter 4

# Simple Energy Techniques (SET)

Over the years, as we worked with clients, we were constantly looking for ways to make EFT more user-friendly and accessible to the average person. We have been very successful in achieving this with our simplified approach, which we call Simple Energy Techniques (SET).

The name says it all, since SET, we believe, is the most practical and easy-to-use meridian energy approach around. As we developed some of the simplifications and refinements of SET, we found this new approach more readily accepted by our clients and workshop participants and, most importantly, clients could *apply* the approach outside of therapy sessions to create improvements in their life. This technique, we found, is one that most people can easily integrate into their daily life. Because it is simple to use, people tend to use it. And it works.

# What is SET?

Simple Energy Techniques (SET) is a collection of simple and user-friendly Energy Techniques, which can provide significant relief for a wide range of emotional problems, and some physical ailments. The main component of SET is the simple process of stimulating energy meridian points on the body for emotional and physical relief. Typically, this involves tapping on the points, but rubbing or simply touching the points can also be used. We also encourage and teach a form of continuous tapping for 'energy toning'. This continual tapping is the cornerstone of SET and is, perhaps, the main element that makes it different to EFT and TFT.

SET is ideal for any condition that has a psychological component. It also functions as a harmonising and integrating force in the 'body–mind' (where the body and the mind are one), which all seems too good to be true in the modern world of stress and anxiety. It brings benefits on many different levels: the habitual levels of unconscious tension; negative attitudes and feelings; and general health and wellbeing. It can also be used for high achievement and conscious planning. Relationships will also generally benefit from the reduced stress this technique can bring.

# The Energy Points of SET

The energy points used in SET include the same upper body and hand points used in EFT. The points used in SET also include the comprehensive points on the top of the head and the wrist points, as introduced by acupuncturist Dr Michael Gandy.

Although SET uses many of the same energy points as EFT, it

eliminates some of the unnecessary steps or encumbering beliefs. Those extra steps are just that — added extras, which can still be used, but only if the basic approach isn't working.

SET does not come under the umbrella of EFT, although it does share a great deal of its basic points. It emphasises meridian stimulation over all else, whether you work indirectly or directly with the technique. On a spectrum from simple to complex, first comes SET, followed by EFT, then for those who want to go further there is our advanced approach, PET (Provocative Energy Techniques). We are not detailing PET in this book because it is more advanced and requires extensive training to be used successfully. However, if you are interested, you can find out more about PET on our website: www.eftdownunder.com.

One of the first things we did when developing SET was to challenge some of the long-standing elements of EFT. These included, among other things:

- The set-up statement and tapping/rubbing the sore spot or karate chop point.
- The concept of psychological reversal (PR).
- The nine-gamut sequence.
- The need for specific sequences of tapping.
- The reminder phrase.
- The need to conduct 'rounds' of tapping.

We have found that you can achieve excellent results without having to follow the 'rules' relating to each of these components of traditional EFT. When we formulated SET we eliminated the set-up statement without any noticeable drop in effectiveness. We also found the use of a reminder phrase to be distracting to many people and encouraged clients to focus on the problem in their own way (although, if you find it helps you to use a reminder phrase, feel free to do so). We simply embraced blocking beliefs as 'the next problem to treat', thus overcoming the need to 'correct for reversal' in most cases and, rather than worrying where to tap or having to conduct 'rounds' of treatment and then stop between each one, we encouraged clients to tap on the points in any order continually throughout the session. We have found that this continual meridian stimulation is one of the most important contributors to positive results.

You can now benefit from many of these refinements which we have trialled and road-tested with a great many clients and thousands of workshop participants. Like them, you'll find you can get results with SET very easily. In fact, we're sure you'll be surprised at how such a simple process can produce such profound results in reducing emotional stress and enhancing your general wellbeing.

## The Cornerstone of SET: Continual Tapping

Continual tapping originated from David's work in treating trauma. 'In the early days I would do a lot of talking about the problem with the client and then we would work through their traumatic incident(s) using EFT. We would typically get through about 10–12 rounds of EFT in a 1-hour session with a lot of talking in between. Later, as I got more efficient, we would get through, say, fifteen rounds of EFT in a session. I noticed that the results were better for clients in those sessions where we had done more rounds of tapping, so I thought, "Why stop? Why not continue tapping throughout the session?" I started doing so, having the client tap not only while relating the story and talking about the problem, but also while processing what happened — basically the whole time during the session. My results improved accordingly.'

David then came up with the concept of tapping on the finger points using the thumb of the same hand. This idea came from observing Dr Larry Nims in his original tapping version of BSFF (Be Set Free Fast) where Dr Nims taught his clients to use the thumb of the same hand to tap on the ring finger and little finger. David took this further and encouraged his clients to tap on all of the fingers using the thumb of the same hand and found this to be a very user-friendly version of tapping. In this version the ring finger, which is left out of the regular EFT sequence because it shares the same meridian as the gamut point, is also included. David began teaching this simple technique to all his clients and had them continually tap on these points during the session, and also whenever they could in-between sessions. The results were excellent.

Since that time we have both experimented with this very simple form of energy-point stimulation and found it not only produces results (through the same meridian stimulation process used in EFT), but it is also more easily adapted and used by clients because it can be done discreetly in public and incorporated into their daily routine.

We now believe that the amount of meridian stimulation conducted is a key factor in producing results.

Continual tapping brings 'quantity' as well as quality, which might matter to the body where, theoretically, the fixed and solid negative patterns live.

Thus, when working with clients in our psychotherapy sessions we now teach them a form of continual tapping where they can tap on any of the meridian points in a continuous fashion throughout the session, even when not specifically focusing on a problem (i.e. even when just 'chatting'). And we tap along with them, which means that we keep our energy clear as well. We find that the increased amount of meridian stimulation is a key factor in improved results and now aim to get as much tapping as possible into every session. The results since we started doing this have been far superior to the time when we just used to do a few rounds of EFT, and discuss things in between rounds.

We preach *persistence* in treatment, exemplified by continual tapping.

# The Main Components of SET

## THE POINTS

SET points include the same energy meridian points as used in EFT, although we don't use the neurolymphatic reflex point (the sore spot), nor do we routinely tap on the gamut point. In SET we also include the side of the ring finger, a point which is not tapped in EFT. Thus, the hand points used in SET incorporate all of the finger points, making it easier to remember.

The hand points are just as helpful to tap on as the upper body points for most people. It is not usually a case of either/or. You can tap on the upper body points when that is convenient and useful, on the hand points when that is convenient and useful, and on all of them if you prefer. You could also tap on the points randomly, or even select just a few of them for tapping (i.e. create your own preferred tapping sequence using all the points you prefer to tap on), and you will typically get results that are just as good as using any particular tapping sequence. This is presumably because the meridian energy points are all ultimately connected, and stimulating one part of the system leads to effects across the entire system. We have found the same thing with SET: the main issue seems to be the amount of energy-point stimulation, rather than where to tap. If you go down the 'where do I tap?' path you will find many conflicting views, all ending in the fact that, when it comes to tapping, 'All roads lead to Rome'.

We encourage you to tap on the energy points in any order or sequence that seems natural to you, and also encourage you to include at least three to four of the points in your sequence. If you find, while doing so, that some points seem to produce extra results, then you might like to include those points more, or tap on them more times than the other points. Develop a sequence that works for you, or simply tap on all of them — whatever your choice, you should expect results.

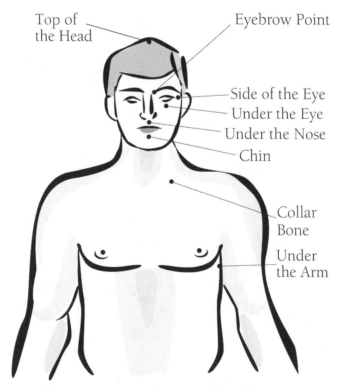

**The energy points used in SET**

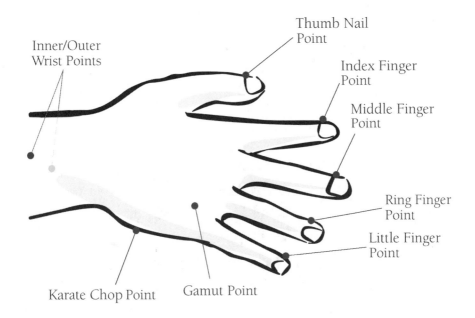

Thumb Nail Point

Inner/Outer Wrist Points

Index Finger Point

Middle Finger Point

Ring Finger Point

Little Finger Point

Karate Chop Point

Gamut Point

## The hand points used in SET

In experimenting with the continual tapping approach, which we now use almost exclusively in SET, we were excited to find that tapping continually on the energy points can relieve even some problems that haven't been tapped on specifically (i.e. when the person doing the tapping has not focused specifically on those issues during the tapping process).

We first noticed this at our 2004 retreat in Broome, Western Australia, when one of the participants found that her lifelong fear of snakes was surprisingly gone three days into the retreat. This was discovered by accident when we attended the Broome markets on a Saturday morning and there was a man there with a large snake. This woman was surprised to find that her phobia had completely gone away, even though we had never specifically focused on the snake phobia in the retreat, nor could anyone identify any point where something related to this may have been discussed. After experimenting continual tapping with the others, we found that the practice seems to have the effect of 'toning' the energy system in a beneficial way, such that many emotional problems can release their hold, even without having been the specific target of the tapping process.

## OMITTING THE SET-UP STATEMENT

Some time ago, we began to experiment with leaving out the set-up statement when doing EFT and found no reduction in effectiveness. Whenever we encountered a blocking belief with clients, instead of doing a regular set-up, we would simply have them tap on the points while focusing on that block and, in most cases, that would lead to progress. Later in this book (see page 81), we will provide more detail regarding this process and how you can use it at home. For now, it is important to point out that we have seen no reduction in effectiveness from discontinuing the routine use of the set-up statement.

So now you don't have to worry about what to say when you are doing the tapping. We encourage you simply to stimulate the energy points while focusing on the problem you want to treat. You can focus on the problem in any way, using whatever you experience naturally. This means using your 'answer' to the question: 'How do I know that I have a problem?' It might be a feeling in the body, or a memory or worry, for example.

On some occasions you might use a statement as a way of framing the problem, however, you do not need to feel constrained in the wording of this or have to tap on any specific point. There is no rule that says the set-up statement must be repeated three times in order to be effective, and results can be achieved without this.

We also see no absolute need to design or repeat a reminder phrase and usually encourage our clients to focus on 'whatever you are aware of' in the mind (thoughts or beliefs) or body (feelings, intensity or bodily location) while you tap. We have found that, for some clients, repeating a reminder phrase may distract them from the feelings or images associated with their problem, rather than helping them 'tune in'.

This means that you can simply tap on the points and focus on the problem in your own way.

## DIRECT AND INDIRECT TAPPING

You can use SET both directly and indirectly. Direct work means you focus on an emotional issue or problem and apply SET to any particular aspects of that problem, especially ones that create emotional intensity for you. Typically this means focusing on either the bodily feelings or emotions, or the thoughts associated with the problem while you tap. As with EFT, if we are focusing on the mind (thoughts) and if things don't seem to be progressing, we will switch to the body (feelings and sensations) and vice versa. You then continue to use SET until the problem no longer affects you emotionally or the intensity of the emotion has significantly reduced. In the simplest terms, this means focusing on the problem and persistently tapping on the SET points until the problem has been resolved.

As with EFT, there may be different aspects of a problem which can upset you, and the aim with direct SET work is to focus on each of these aspects in turn (or as they arise) while tapping or rubbing the SET energy points, until you are emotionally clear and calm with all of the aspects being treated.

A useful and simple model for direct work using SET is to go for a walk (or another activity) for 20–30 minutes, and let your mind roam around the problem you want to work on directly. Allow your thoughts to come up in a natural and 'conversational' way while you use continual tapping. In particular, allow the negative and bleak things some space on your mental stage; tapping does give you the freedom to do this without excessive suffering. You could also focus on the body feelings that come up, as well as any thoughts, memories or ideas. If you felt like ruminating, you could do that. If you felt like making positive affirmations, you could do that too. It is important to note that in both cases you are actually working on the negativity (either directly with the negative, or indirectly in the sense of what is 'not being thought or said because it is opposite' in using the positive). Additional tapping, when the problem is 'attuned' by way of being intense, often brings major relief. Then, when time is up, just get on with what you were doing in your day, knowing you can always have another 'session' later. In this way, you can stay detached from the emotional 'heat' of the problem.

In indirect SET, you simply stimulate the SET points by tapping or rubbing on them without concern for what you are thinking or feeling. We recommend you do this on a daily basis, as a form of emotional fitness. As incredible as it may sound, we have found that this very simple process of just stimulating the energy points regularly (i.e. for just a few minutes each day) can have very beneficial results for many people. Most of these benefits are connected to a process we call *energy toning*. This is a process where the positive effects of stimulating the energy points seem to accumulate in your system, like a positive form of emotional fitness.

It's easy to incorporate the practice of continual tapping into your daily routine because it generally does not require you to stop anything you are doing. In particular, if you are using the fingertip tapping process of tapping the thumb on the fingers of the same hand, it is discreet and easy to use socially, for example, while on the telephone, reading, doing computer work, or walking. Remember that you can also just hold or rub the points discreetly if you are feeling conspicuous for any reason, and that will also work well. It promotes relaxation and stress relief at the same time.

In addition, we have found that when you tap on the energy points on a regular basis (such as for 15 minutes or more each day over a period of at least 1–2 weeks), then a beneficial effect tends to accumulate over time. In fact, it seems that many of the benefits of the tapping treatment occur on several levels at once. When practised daily for several weeks, just using the energy-toning effects of tapping alone are enough to induce an experience of calm, and a kind of 'emotional fitness' for most people. Daily practice also maintains the benefits of the tapping treatment.

We've found that about an hour a day (made up of smaller time periods added together) is very beneficial, although any tapping can often bring calm. When you link it to your ordinary daily activities (like watching TV), you will easily have enough tapping in your day.

What are you thinking about while you do this? *Nothing.* It is an indirect approach meant to settle your body's reactivity down. We have had many examples of clients and workshop participants using regular daily tapping who found that some of their emotional problems 'just went away' of their own accord, and the severity of emotions linked to other issues reduced significantly over time. In addition, many reported an increase in positive emotions and a general feeling of optimism associated with life in general.

Again, these benefits of daily tapping can occur *even when you tap without focusing on any of your emotional problems*. Simply tap on the points as you go about your business, and allow the benefits to accumulate, just as you would if you were going to the gym every day (only you don't have to go to the gym to do this, you can do the tapping virtually anytime, anywhere!).

**Linking Tapping to a Problem**

Here is a very simple, yet effective, indirect way for you to work with any problem: Allow your 'problem' (thought or feeling) to be what it is and just 'graft' the tapping on top of it while it is present.

In this way you never struggle with what is, nor do you set up any further tension by wishing or hoping or arguing with yourself about your issue. Often a negative problem causes great secondary tensions as your beliefs and preferences and values are triggered. In essence, we suggest that you tap on your problem as and when you feel it without modifying it at all. It is a way of saying 'yes' to the problem without having to resist it, because it is often that very resistance that causes problems to persist.

This is an ideal first step when dealing with issues. This strategy has the merit of instant action and provides a 'defusing' function. It is very do-able, portable, and a good 'habit' to get into, and the benefits are threefold:

- You are doing something useful and helpful by tapping.

- Most likely the reactions will settle down. You are not making the problem worse by over-reacting — this is more likely when you don't think about it too much! (By this we mean there is less inner debate about whether the problem should have happened, or why it happened now, or is it fair, or who is really to blame etc.).

- You are interrupting the pattern of your own negative reactions just at the right time.

72

Remember that tapping is foremost a body technique — not a direct psychological one — so the Energy Techniques answer 'problems' that you feel must also lie in the body. You don't have to allow the mind to get over-involved too soon unless it's appropriate, particularly in self-help situations. By grafting tapping to the problem, you can use tapping in a particular way that is both indirect and powerful, but you don't have to make a big mental effort.

In fact, it is common when working on one problem directly (e.g. a phobia), to find that other similar or associated problems have settled down dramatically *without ever being addressed specifically*. And most likely, other positive changes by association over time will occur in your self-confidence and self-esteem, along with a reduction in chronic forms of tension. Over the years, we've seen that the benefits of indirect tapping can often be every bit as good as that of direct and focused tapping, and that the ongoing effects of continual tapping may last for many hours.

Is there any drawback to using SET in an indirect way? Unfortunately, the indirect method might look too trivial to help, and your mind might refuse to accept the idea of just 'toning and tuning' the body. However, you can always use the direct method anytime you feel like it. Either way can be effective — as long as you tap.

## USING THE RIGHT WORDS IN SET

It's common to be concerned about getting the instructions correct (and worried about getting them 'wrong'). But, in SET, you might not need any words at all! While EFT/SET are both robust and forgiving as techniques, it's easy to forget that they are first and foremost body–energy techniques (they work on the energy system in the body), and not strictly psychological techniques.

Rather than getting anxious when trying to figure out what to say, we find it better to keep it simple at first, and just tap while focusing on your body sensations and reactions. Later you can get into the direct and indirect methods, explore limiting beliefs, alternate positive and negative elements of the issue, and have fun playing with more provocative ways of exploring your thoughts, opinions, beliefs and emotions. We'll explain more about that later.

## SET and Self-Help

The general processes of using SET for self-help are simple and effective. Firstly, focus SET on any emotional or physical problem and simply tap on any of the points in any order until you feel relief. If you prefer you can rub or hold the points — just get some meridian stimulation happening. The actual sequence you use doesn't matter all that much, although it does seem necessary to include at least three to four different meridian points in the sequence.

Even when you aren't specifically focusing on the problem, just tap on the points continually (remember, continual tapping with one hand is very convenient). This appears to have the beneficial effect of 'toning' your energy system. It works even if you are not actually concentrating directly (although directly is ideal), or you don't know consciously what the problem is. Tap to allow your 'body–mind' to function smoothly, without your having to think.

Next try to get some meridian stimulation into your day wherever possible, without always worrying about having to say or do anything specific. Most people who do this on a daily basis report that their levels of optimism and positive energy increase over time and that their general stress levels decrease. We now believe that enough meridian stimulation may cause a positive shift in your nervous system such that your negative problems cannot take hold in the same way.

We also recommend linking continual tapping to other habits such as watching TV, talking on the phone or going for a walk. Make it a beneficial habit. In addition, don't just wait for a problem to arise to start tapping. By tapping on a regular basis (say up to 1 hour in total per day), you will be increasing your positive energy and decreasing your stress levels automatically.

It is fine to also do focused or direct sessions where you aim to specifically target the aspects of your problem and apply energy stimulation (tapping or rubbing the points) to them. Consider working with someone else if you have trouble identifying parts of the problem to work on. In the meantime, continual tapping without specific focusing can still be beneficial.

Let your thoughts and feelings come while you tap. Accept every thought and feeling — and allow even negative thoughts to come — but add tapping to their presence ('graft it on to the problem'). You *will* interrupt those patterns.

Take a deep breath after a sequence of tapping or when you notice a 'shift'.

Finally, be willing to consult a professional therapist or physician for more complex issues that don't shift, especially for undiagnosed physical issues.

## HOW DO ENERGY TECHNIQUES WORK?

The way tapping on energy points (as used in EFT/SET) brings results is not entirely known. There are interesting theories about where the negative emotions spring from, and how. Obviously, something radical is happening if tapping on body energy points removes pain, anxiety and fear so effectively — even if sceptics suppose that the process is 'all in the mind', or due to some kind of mental conditioning!

If we entertain the theory that tapping works because it is a direct mental focus, then we shouldn't expect to see results when we think of nothing and just make tapping a pleasant and relaxing habit. But with indirect tapping that's exactly what we do see ... and we experience results time and time again. As David recalls:

> 'My daily experience of a gnawing, empty feeling in the "stomach" as a response to any fear or anxiety significantly decreased after the first six months of using tapping extensively. Some months later I realised that it had just disappeared! It has never returned — despite repeated provocation. I don't miss it. This amounts to a physiological shift in an automatic nervous reactivity. I still have my commonsense and caution, but I no longer seem to need a body "alarm system" that never really helped me anyway. Now I use continual tapping whenever I am "below par", or in a contracted state, or can't think clearly. Or just because I like to do so.'

If we go with a physiological approach to tapping, since the essence of acupuncture is continual point stimulation, then point stimulation may be a useful bridge between acupuncture and acupressure, and therefore lead to the results of tapping.

Using this theory, much of the energy toning effect comes from somehow disrupting your body's capacity to express the feeling of some negative emotion. Most of these problems seem to manifest as uncomfortable feelings in the midline of the body, often around the nerve plexuses (such as the solar plexus). We've seen that enough tapping can remarkably reduce or even eliminate some 'nervous reactions' felt in these areas. Could it be that the tapping upsets the pathways for pain in the body that are formed when we have negative emotional reactions and hurts?

If you can inhibit that expression over time by tapping (either directly or indirectly), then where is your feeling of having the problem? Where is the negative distress? It is not there — or at least you can't and don't perceive it. So the tapping might settle your body down at a deep level and somehow change the final expressive pathway of feeling any problem's distress. Now here's the fascinating part: is the problem still there according to this way of looking at it? Yes. Is the distress about the problem still there? No.

This is where two astonishing implications come in:

- **Is it possible to separate an emotional problem or phobia from the 'upset' of it?**

- **Could we handle a problem better once we've decreased or eliminated the distress of it?**

In our experience, and in the experiences of our many clients over the years, and all over the world, the answer to both these questions is a resounding YES.

## Tackling Blocking Beliefs With SET

As with EFT, there may be times when you fail to progress with SET, or your progress only reaches a certain point and then stops. Similarly to EFT, the usual reasons for this are the presence of additional aspects or blocking beliefs.

To review, aspects are other parts of a problem, and all of these parts may need treatment in order for you to get full relief. Aspects may be different ways the problem affects you, such as related feelings, and/or different bodily sensations; different images associated with the problem (such as visual versus auditory elements, or different visual images); or different events or places where you experience the problem. Typically, persistence is the best way to treat aspects.

If you are working specifically with SET, then you want to focus on each of the aspects of the problem that cause you intensity until they no longer affect you. In SET, this simply means focusing on each aspect 'in your own way' and tapping on the points while you do so. Sometimes, aspects come up on their own, in which case you just keep on tapping until you get to a position of calm on the problem. At other times, you need to search for all of the parts of the problem that cause you emotional angst and apply continual tapping while focusing on each aspect until that aspect no longer bothers you. Keep persisting through the aspects until you reach a position of calm on each part of the problem you are treating.

## TREAT ANGER AT YOURSELF

It is almost universally true that we are angry at ourselves in some way for having the problems that we do, even if this makes no sense logically, or we are angry at the fact that we aren't handling our problems better. In addition to treating any blocking beliefs, it is important to treat any anger that you have at yourself for having the problem.

Self-anger can often be treated by simply conducting a minute or two of SET tapping while focusing on the idea: 'I am angry at myself for having this problem or for not handling it better.' This self-anger can also relate to a belief about what you should have done, or about how you should be handling the problem or issue. If you can identify this 'should' belief, it can often be treated by a minute or two of SET continual tapping.

## TREATING BLOCKING BELIEFS

So, what is a belief? Much has been written about the power of our beliefs to create or destroy our lives, to mould our lives, to produce and limit our results, or to create our very reality. Yet, a belief may be nothing more than an idea attached to strong feelings — an idea to which we have become emotionally attached by our conditioning either through a few specific events or a large number of emotionally charged events over time. It could be thought of as an association or link that has become secure through repetition or through strong emotional connections. We all have positive and negative beliefs that influence how we behave in everyday life, and it is the negative ones that we seek to treat in SET.

There are many common blocking beliefs that can get in the way of effective treatment. As mentioned previously, in EFT these beliefs are usually addressed by inserting a belief statement into the set-up statement, then conducting a round or two of tapping while repeating the belief as a statement at each point. For example, if your belief was 'I'm not good enough' you would simply repeat this statement at each tapping point while tapping. This is because, according to EFT theory, the psychological reversal (PR) caused by the belief needs to be treated, and the set-up statement is presumed necessary to do this.

One of the things we did when developing SET was to challenge some of the assumptions behind EFT. One of the main ones was the need for a set-up statement to move past blocks or to deal with blocking beliefs. In SET, instead of constructing a set-up statement, you simply tap on the points while focusing on your problem.

What if you are not making progress when applying SET tapping? What we have found is that any block can most easily be overcome by treating the block itself as *the next problem to treat*. Then you simply tap on the energy points while focusing on the block itself. *Blocks to progress almost always represent blocking beliefs.*

However, the good news is that, in order to progress beyond a block (or belief) using SET, it isn't necessary, in many cases, to even know exactly what the blocking belief is. If you encounter a block or inner resistance or find that you are failing to progress, you can, for example, simply tap on the points and focus on 'this block' or 'whatever is holding me back from getting over this problem', and then just tap on the points as you do so and see where this takes you. Often things will start to move after this.

If you are able to identify the relevant blocking belief then you simply focus on that belief — however you are aware of it mentally, physically and emotionally — and tap on the SET points. For example, if you are tapping for your fear of flying and the thought comes into your mind that 'I will never get over this problem because it is too severe', then you focus on that thought and tap on the points. If, when thinking that thought you become aware of a feeling in your body, then make that feeling the focus of your tapping and continue tapping until the feeling shifts.

The problem, however, is that many of our blocking beliefs are unconscious. This is why, as mentioned in the chapter on EFT, it can be helpful to tap while focusing on some common blocking beliefs.

What you might try first if you're failing to progress, or if your progress has stalled, is running through a list of the common blocking beliefs to see if treating these enhances your results. Any of the beliefs outlined in the EFT section on 'Psychological Reversal' (see page 54) may also be treated using SET. Feel free to consult that list and apply to them the simple SET process outlined below or, if you prefer, use the summary of most common blocking beliefs also provided below as a shortcut.

### How to Apply SET to a Blocking Belief

Once again, the wonderful thing about using SET is that, in order to treat these blocking beliefs effectively, you don't need to insert them into a set-up statement. If you have identified a belief that is blocking your progress, you simply focus on it in your own way while tapping continually on the energy points. Do this for 2–3 minutes or until you notice a shift in either thinking or feeling, then go back to the problem you are addressing and focus on it again and apply continual tapping. In most cases you will find your tapping work pays dividends.

By applying SET to the emotionally connected idea itself — the belief statement or association — you can begin the process of decreasing your emotional attachment to it. As soon as you identify a belief you can tap on it. For example, if your belief is 'I am stupid', you would tap on the energy points while focusing on or repeating the negative belief statement 'I am stupid' at each tapping point. Since tapping works on the negatives when you are treating negative beliefs, you want to tap on the negative belief *as you perceive it*, in other words, exactly how you think and feel it inside, if you want to get maximum effects. You may also want to work on all of the related beliefs and ideas — the negative thoughts that go with the 'I am stupid' belief — and state these out loud as you tap on each of the points (e.g. 'I'm dumb', 'I am a slow learner', 'I am a bad . . .'). If you can exaggerate these statements as you tap on them, it can help to reduce the emotional intensity, as getting results with SET does not require maximum intensity.

It isn't as much the truth of a belief as it is how intense this belief makes you feel, and the limiting emotional effects of it in your life, that is the real problem. For example, if you have a belief that 'I can't swim' and you have never learned to swim because you are fearful of drowning, then that belief may be a statement of truth in present time. Therefore treating this belief with Energy Techniques won't make you instantly able to go out and swim the English Channel! What it will do is leave you open to being able to learn to swim, should you find this useful, and remove any blocks to your being able to move forward. The goal is to relax any negative feelings associated with this issue, making you feel more comfortable in and around water. This means you can move forward without being blocked — you are then emotionally free on this issue.

Here again are some of the blocking beliefs that are commonly present:

'I don't believe I can get over this problem.'

'It's too hard for me to get over this problem.'

'It's not safe for me to get over this problem.'

'I don't deserve to get over this problem.'

'This problem is a part of me.'

'I'll be a different person if I get over this problem.'

If you just can't seem to make any progress, then the following belief may be operating: 'I can't get completely over this problem.'

Use the process outlined above and see if you can make progress on your problem. Sometimes the above beliefs can be connected. For example, someone who has had a traumatic experience may believe that they won't be safe if they completely get over their fear and anxiety. A person who has been in a car accident may feel a certain amount of anxiety every time they get into a vehicle. A minute or two of continual tapping on one or more of the following belief statements may help you to get some progress on this issue:

'It's not safe for me to get over this problem.'

'It's not safe for me to get completely over this problem.'

'I'm afraid to get over this problem.'

When the fear-related belief has been treated sufficiently then the fear feelings are usually able to pass through the mind–body and the person realises that these negative feelings did not really serve them at all.

If you are using SET with other people, one belief that is often important to address is the client's belief that they cannot get results without the counsellor's or therapist's assistance. Again, sometimes just focusing in on the client's negative belief statement and conducting a minute or two of SET continual tapping can be enough to address this belief. When this doesn't happen, consider that the underlying problem may be deeper, such as low self-esteem, and follow the more detailed approach for treating beliefs as outlined below.

**Where Did You Learn This Belief?**
A third way of treating blocking beliefs is to identify where you learned them and apply EFT/SET to those emotionally charged events. Good questions to ask here are:

'Where did I first learn this?'

'Who taught me this?'

'What does this remind me of?'

Once you have identified the significant emotional experiences, you can set about treating these by using the 'Tell the Story' technique. This technique, which is explained in more detail in Chapter 6 (see page 120) basically involves going through the story and identifying any emotionally intense parts of it, then applying EFT/SET to those aspects until they reduce. You then continue the process until you get through the entire story and can tell it without any remaining emotional intensity. If you do this systematically with the major life events behind your current belief, you will almost certainly feel shifts in your own attachment to this belief, such that the belief is less strongly held.

*If you are dealing with highly traumatic events and very strongly held beliefs, you should consider working through these with a qualified practitioner and therapist.*

### An Example of Applying SET to a Common Blocking Belief

Let's say you have a fear of being in enclosed spaces like elevators or planes. To begin, you focus on the fear, and one way of doing this is to bring to mind the places and situations where this fear arises. Start off by thinking about being in an elevator or sitting in a plane and this 'tunes you in' to the negative feeling. Next, tap continually on the SET points until the fear feeling reduces, or another aspect arises, then continue until you have no remaining emotional intensity. Although it is possible to tap on the SET points in any order, it can help when you are starting to use a standard sequence where you start at the top of your body and go down. Begin by tapping on the top of your head, followed by the eyebrow, side of the eye, under the eye, under the chin, collarbone and then on the thumb point and each of the finger points, finishing on the wrist points (see diagrams on pages 66 and 67). Next take a deep breath and check your level of emotional intensity. In this case, let's say you are tapping away while thinking about being in an elevator and you aren't noticing any shifts at all; in fact, your fear feels the same even after several minutes of tapping. The first thing to know is that often persistence will pay off for such issues, and a lot of tapping may ultimately be required in order for you to achieve full relief. However, it is common to feel something within the first few minutes of doing the tapping, if only to notice that your mind wants to focus on another part of the problem. If, however, you suspect you have a block or you feel that nothing is happening, then it can help to focus your tapping towards that block.

Let's say, in this case, you don't know what the block is, but what you do know is that the tapping isn't leading to one bit of relief. Focus your tapping either on the thoughts that have arisen in your mind, such as 'This isn't working' or 'This obviously won't work for me', or whatever else you are aware of in your thinking, or simply tap for 'This block' as mentioned before. If you have a feeling of frustration or other feeling associated with the belief, you can focus on that as you tap.

Another way of working on this issue is to go through the list of common blocking beliefs (see page 55) and try some tapping while focusing on each of them in turn. Remember, when treating blocking beliefs using SET it isn't essential to use a set-up statement as in EFT. Instead, simply focus on the belief and tap on the points. For example, a blocking belief that may apply here is the belief that you won't be safe if you get over this problem. One way to treat this is to focus on this belief, or simply repeat it to yourself in your mind or out loud, while you tap on the points. Once you have done this for a few minutes, you can then focus back on the fear of enclosed spaces and you will generally find that things start to move at this point. If not, try tapping on another of the common blocking beliefs from the list and, if necessary, go through each of them in turn.

## GOING DEEPER IN TREATING BLOCKING BELIEFS

For beliefs that resist the simple approach of tapping while focusing on the belief statement, it may be necessary to identify and treat the specific events where these beliefs were learned.

Again, using the example above, you may have learned that it was unsafe to be in enclosed spaces through some negative past experience (e.g. finding yourself locked in, or being forcibly held by a bigger, more aggressive person, or some other situation where you linked enclosed places to painful emotions). In such cases, it can help to bring these past events up in your mind and treat them using the 'Run the Movie' or 'Tell the Story' techniques which we explain in detail in Chapter 6 (see page 120).

But there's something even better we need to mention at this point. You can also use this process to treat beliefs that have been holding you back in your life generally, such as a negative belief about yourself (that you are not good enough or 'stupid'), or a belief about success, such as 'Success is hard work'. And when the emotional connections associated with these negative beliefs are disconnected using a process like EFT/SET, then the belief becomes just an idea amidst the great sea of ideas. You could say it returns to the great sea of ideas, and even though we can still think it, the idea no longer has a hold on us: it no longer affects us and no longer drives our feelings and behaviour.

In the sections to come, we will address this and show you how these restricting beliefs can be treated and, ultimately, shifted using Energy Techniques. That way you can free yourself for the success you deserve.

## HOW DO WE WORK WITH OUR VALUES USING EFT/SET?

A particular type of belief that can often hold us back is our values. Values are the emotional states we consider the most important to experience or avoid. It could be argued that all of our actions are ultimately designed to achieve the emotional states we value most (i.e. associate most pleasure with) and avoid the emotional states we associate the most pain with. Values are the key to our decisions and often there's a conflict between them where, for example, we may value security but also value challenge. Typically, the value with the strongest emotional attachments (often learned in childhood) will be the one that drives our decisions and actions.

For example, if you've learned to value security very highly because the environment you grew up in was very insecure, then you'll have a hard time getting yourself to take risks, even if you know intellectually that to do so will greatly improve your situation. Ironing out these conflicts using EFT/SET can be a very rewarding exercise, and can free up a tremendous amount of energy to achieve your goals. Using SET you can iron out conflicts in your values, where two opposing values are pulling you in different directions. Once you've done this you're ultimately more easily able to live a life congruent with your highest values, thus freeing you to live out your own version of success.

# Chapter 5

# General Applications of EFT/SET

Now that you know the basics of EFT/SET, let's look at how you can apply these techniques to improve your life. In this chapter we will look at general applications, such as how to use tapping to get the best results, and how to use it with other people.

## Four Powerful Ways to Use Energy Techniques

**REMEDIAL**

This is where we use EFT/SET to clear out problems, fix phobias, overcome past traumas, and create shifts on the emotional problems that we face. The remedial level is where most people who are using Energy Techniques with their clients will start, since clients come to us in pain and want a shift in their emotional problems. It is also the level where many people who are hurting will seek help, and where a self-helper will focus their attention.

Unfortunately, for many people this is as far as they will go with these energy treatments and that's a shame because there is much, much more that can be achieved. Some of the best uses of these techniques will be found when we move beyond the remedial level.

## PREVENTATIVE

This is where you don't just treat current symptoms, but you also look towards the future and apply tapping to that in order to ensure that you 'have all the bases covered'. You might consider all of the situations where the problem might arise, and treat yourself for each of them ahead of time. If you had a public speaking fear, for example, you might tap while focusing, in turn, on all the different things that might stir you up about a future public speaking event. You might imagine types of speaking situations that you will encounter, such as having to use a microphone, having to speak 'off-the-cuff', or being asked a question you don't know the answer to.

The remedial and preventative levels are excellent to work on and powerful results can be gained; however, our work is incomplete if we don't move beyond this to the creative/generative level.

## CREATIVE/GENERATIVE

This is where we consider alternative possible futures that we wish to create and apply tapping to the process of being that, doing that and achieving that. Here, tapping is used as a tool to assist us to manifest our positive intentions and create the life we want. We tap to merge with our intention, raise our vibration, get comfortable with what is outside our current comfort zone, and access the energy and feeling of success.

'Connecting with Success', a process which will be explained in more detail later in Chapter 6 (see page 187), is an exciting process which involves imagining the ideal that you want to create or achieve while simultaneously tapping on the energy points. You tap while vividly imagining how that ideal will really feel. Progressively, as you do this, the images and feelings tend to feel and become more real. In our experience in working with peak performers, just one moment of true connection with those feelings is superior to hundreds of affirmations or visualisations of success without the feeling.

Creative tapping and 'Connecting with Success' should be combined with 'remedial work' for best results. As you tap, objections, blocking beliefs and negative feelings will arise — these can be perfect targets for your remedial and preventative tapping sessions. Initially, regular tapping sessions of the creative/generative kind should be performed separately from the remedial tapping sessions; however, both will be required overall. A rush to the generative level may result in a lack of validation and rapport, and could also push the problem areas back underground. A balance of approaches usually provides the best overall results.

We will also provide more detail on the process of tapping for creative change later in this book (see page 203).

## ENERGY TONING

As we've mentioned previously, tapping for energy toning involves conducting the tapping as a daily discipline or positive practice. The simple process of continually tapping on the energy points in any order for a period of time each day (say from 15 minutes to 1 hour) often leads to disproportionate positive results. Continual tapping on the meridian points, even without specific focus, appears to have the effect of 'toning' the energy system in a beneficial way such that many emotional problems can be found to progressively release their hold — even if they haven't been specifically targeted or focused on. This regular tapping tends to have the effect of increasing positive energy and decreasing stress levels at the same time. We recommend linking continual tapping to other habits such as watching TV, talking on the phone or going for a walk, so that the tapping becomes integrated into your regular routine. Make it a habit!

# How to Use EFT/SET in Public

One of the most frequently asked questions at our workshops and by our clients is: 'What happens if my problem occurs when I am out in public?'

Obviously, most people are going to feel nervous about tapping on points on their face and body while out in public, as this looks rather strange. And that can be an issue because many of our emotional problems actually occur when we are in public places. Here Steve has an example:

'I remember way back in February 1998, after attending Gary Craig's "Steps Towards Becoming the Ultimate Therapist" Workshop, sitting in a San Francisco café tapping away on the EFT points after a 1-hour bus ride sitting next to a woman with strong perfume had left me with a severe headache. David sat next to me, tapping along. A street beggar came along, took one look at us, and gave us a wide berth! Although the headache went away, and the petrochemical sensitivity has also almost totally dissipated since that *time, that incident reminded me how strange the tapping process can appear to members of the general public!'*

Over the years we have come up with the following advice if you have a problem that occurs in public places, or if you find yourself in a public place needing to tap.

## TAP BEFORE YOU GO

Obviously the best possible outcome is to not have your problem come up in a public space in its most intense form. This means that if you have a problem, such as anxiety, that is likely to be provoked by being in a public situation, the best thing to do is to think about all the situations where the anxiety might occur ahead of time and tap while focusing on those possibilities. At the very least this can often reduce the intensity of the emotion, if it does happen, to a more manageable level. If you are able to get to the point where you can think about being in the situation (i.e. speaking in public) and thinking about it doesn't produce any emotion, there is a good chance that when you go out either the emotion won't occur or it will be at a lesser level.

## TAP 'AS YOU GO'

Let's say you have a fear of public speaking and you have to give a speech at your friend's wedding. During the days leading up to the event you will have tapped while imagining yourself at the wedding reception giving the speech; you will have tried to identify all the various aspects of speaking in public that might provoke your fear and applied tapping to them; and you would have applied tapping to emotionally intense past speaking events. You can also tap as you get ready to attend the event and on the way to the event.

## EXCUSE YOURSELF

If it's possible, you can excuse yourself from the situation and go off somewhere private to do some tapping. This may mean, for example, dashing to the toilet just before your speech and getting in a few rounds of tapping. Usually this will be sufficient to reduce your anxiety to a more manageable level.

## TOUCHING OR RUBBING THE POINTS

If you have done the remedial, preventative and creative/generative steps and you still have anxiety when you get into the situation, or your anxiety arises 'out of the blue' while out in public, you can try lightly touching or rubbing on some of the points. Often this can be done quite unobtrusively and a few light rubs on selected points can take the edge off the anxiety so that you can function in the situation. If you have done a lot of EFT or SET at home, often just rubbing on the first point in the sequence can initiate a significant shift in intensity.

## YOUR FAVOURITE POINT

After you have been tapping for a while, it is common to identify a favourite point which produces quite large shifts for you. Often, instead of needing to do a full sequence of tapping, just tapping a few times on this point can produce a major shift in intensity. Once you have identified a point such as this, it can be quite handy if you have only a few seconds before you have to perform in public to just tap a few times on that point, or when out in public to just lightly rub the point in a non-obvious way.

## THE FINGER POINTS

The finger points can be tapped under the table or behind your back, however, the best way we have found to do this is to use the thumb of the same hand to tap on the finger points of that hand. This process can be done quite easily out in public and is very unobtrusive. It can also be done under the table or behind the back without being noticed. Even when done publicly most people don't pay much attention to it. Once on an aeroplane we noticed a gentleman absently tapping on these points — and he didn't even know SET! A golfer Steve once worked with had discovered that if she tapped on these points after a bad shot it would reduce her tension prior to the next shot.

## IMAGINE THE TAPPING

It is often possible to get a significant reduction in emotional intensity just by 'imagining' that you are tapping on the points. In one of our workshops, a woman overcame her life-long phobia of spiders just by imagining that she was tapping on the points, with no physical tapping at all! It seems strange to many people that this can work, but our experience is that around 80 per cent of people can get a result from imaginary tapping without needing any further instruction! Try it and see. You may be surprised. It is easy to believe that we can point a remote control at a television to get it to turn on, why should it be surprising that we can use our own intention to produce a result in our own mind–body?

# How to Apply EFT/SET to Yourself

It can be quite productive to write a journal while sitting in front of a computer doing EFT/SET. You can begin by typing out a description of the challenge, problem, negative thought, negative belief or behaviour that you want to work on. Then simply do a minute or two of SET (continual tapping) on that problem. As more thoughts and feelings come up, type these onto the screen. (Previous to our developing SET we would do rounds of EFT, which also works, although we have found that the continual tapping of SET tends to allow us to flow more easily with the thoughts and feelings that arise.)

You can type quite quickly as you work through various aspects of your problem and feel the shifts that occur literally before your eyes. Whether the aspects that come up are feelings, memories, thoughts or belief statements, you type them onto the screen and then include them in a new tapping sequence.

As you type, you may gain greater clarity and a conscious understanding of your issues and find that the subsequent tapping you do is a bit more focused and therefore more productive. Although typing onto the screen works for many people because they can do so rapidly, if you write faster than you type; or if you simply prefer to write, you could complete notes in a paper journal as you tap through the various aspects.

We find the best feature of this approach occurs at the end of the tapping session. When you go back over the material you have typed onto the screen you get to see just how far you have moved from where you began. Often you will be amazed at just how much ground can be covered, and you will also be gratified to find that the issues or aspects you started with will no longer bother you.

We have found that in regular tapping sessions, a person's natural tendency is to just move onto the next aspect that comes up. As the previous aspects drop naturally from our consciousness it is easy to forget that we were quite upset when we first sat down to tap. Many times we haven't realised the full benefit of our regular tapping sessions until long after the fact when we confront a situation that would otherwise have upset us and find it doesn't any longer. We're sure this situation is familiar to many who do this kind of tapping on a regular basis.

The journalising process overcomes these challenges, and not only assists you in clarifying aspects as you go, but also allows you to realise and celebrate the changes you have made immediately after you make them. We find this immediate feedback on results to be a very gratifying element of the approach and we recommend it to everyone who wants to go further in their tapping sessions.

## Tapping On Other People

When, in your moment of need, you feel the benefits of EFT/SET because somebody you trust is tapping on your points, it is a wonderful feeling. But how do we know when this is right or appropriate?

Some situations are so 'right' that EFT or SET for others is natural and helpful (e.g. a parent using it for a child in need, and for most children under the age of eight). Gary Craig, in his EFT teaching workshops, routinely taps on other people's points because he prefers to do so, and because he has explicit permission. The results of one partner tapping on another when dealing with the irritations of being a couple can be very healing. However, although it is easy to tap on other people, we prefer to teach EFT/SET primarily as self-help, and to use them on other people thoughtfully. In our society today all therapeutic touch is suspect legally, so we need to have the best intention, framework, ethics and rapport when doing this deliberately.

It is right to be cautious even when the situation requires EFT/SET, since we can never be sure how our actions will be perceived — it might be an unwanted intrusion into the other person's inner world. While EFT/SET will often be healing in this situation, it is also empowering when a client learns that self-help with EFT/SET nearly always works too.

In our teaching workshops we explicitly ask for permission to tap on the participants, which means informed consent for the helper to touch the client on the hand or wrist points, or sometimes the accessible face points, if necessary. This is a good model for private work too.

Many feelings are just pure 'hurt' and cause a temporary thinking incapacity. Because energy-point stimulation, as used in EFT/SET, is the antidote here, it is important to keep tapping through the intense feelings. If a client in private practice is feeling such emotion that they are unable to concentrate, then with permission we may help them by doing their tapping for them on their points until they have recovered sufficiently to resume. These situations are sporadic in our experience and don't usually last very long — typically only a minute or two.

It's tempting to 'do EFT/SET' for others because it seems to add an extra dimension of intention and energy exchange. David personally attributes the results of his public speaking phobia treatment from a session with Gary Craig, where Gary frequently tapped on David. We both do it for our families, too. But we would always be thoughtful about doing this for others without a specific understanding together.

# The Challenge of Using EFT/SET Consistently

Sometimes, the internal resistance to doing something unfamiliar is strong. The resistance to doing something that is either good for you, or helpful to you, is also strong (this is the human condition). Then there is inertia, laziness and procrastination. We 'forget' to tap, and we also forget how good the results can be! In addition, many people cannot be their own therapist for deeper issues (the unconscious is, of course, unconscious) so when the problems are too close to us, or cannot be named, there is a natural reluctance to change things. Very typically when someone reports little progress with Energy Techniques, they are not having enough stimulation in the right way.

We prefer to think about energy-point stimulation as the general approach. If you take away the concept of the set-up statement as used in EFT, then things seem a lot easier, because a potent cause of uncertainty is 'What do I say, and what am I really feeling or tapping on anyway?' A large part of the benefit of EFT/SET is having that meridian stimulation occur while the problem is represented in the body as a feeling. No words or thoughts are necessary in this simple level of tapping. So the more meridian stimulation you do, the better the associated relaxation and side benefit of helping the 'unknown' (unconscious) issues. We have not seen this persistent tapping exhaust or bother anyone.

One of the best ways we find to address deeper issues is to identify them and focus on them while going for a walk, while using the continual tapping process previously outlined. You tune into the different levels of the problem in a conversational and natural way, knowing that the tapping energy is available to you. And you are multi-tasking with your body!

Of course, there are programs offering dedicated tapping on specific issues, such as weight loss regimes, which take the decision-making out of self-help to a large degree and provide more hand-holding, if this is desirable. But even without knowing all about a problem intellectually, we can be confident that there are ways to release blocks *that we are not even aware of* by simply tapping a lot. You can also tap on 'not tapping enough' or 'forgetting to tap' or 'being stuck'. Are we having fun yet?

In a subtle way the 'generalising effect' of EFT/SET becomes more readily apparent over several weeks, and then most people typically want more of that good feeling.

## SOME ADDITIONAL SUGGESTIONS

Rather than making EFT or SET an interruption that we need to find time for, we need to find ways to integrate it into our daily life. Getting enough energy-point stimulation happening, by finding a way to just tap on various points throughout the day, can often lead to an improvement in your overall state that persists.

When Steve set out to conduct his 30-day self-acceptance trial using EFT (see page 147) one of the first thoughts that came to him was, 'I won't follow through with this.' So he immediately did some tapping while thinking this thought and experiencing the associated feeling, and was pleasantly surprised to find that the next day he actually felt like doing it. Thus, we recommend tapping while focusing on any of your blocking thoughts and feelings as a first step, and any other objections you have to following through on doing the tapping.

We have written previously about how we tend to limit our uses of EFT/SET to a few narrow areas, and don't always think to use these techniques expansively. Because we often tend to see EFT/SET as just remedial tools for 'fixing' negative emotion, rather than as tools for enhancing our life, we don't always keep in mind what they really can do for us.

# Why Don't EFT/SET 'Work' On Some Serious Disorders?

If we knew exactly why EFT/SET worked in the first place, then the mechanics of these techniques wouldn't be a theory (taking their place alongside the theory of psychoanalysis, and the theory of relativity). We might also know more about why they occasionally did not work.

But, despite their unknown mechanics, in our experience there is no disorder on which EFT/SET have had no effect at all in, at least, some individuals or with some manifestations. The definition of a treatment 'working' is broad, but according to our definition it means:

*A significant resolution of the distress accompanying your problem, so that it no longer affects you emotionally.*

So, in this respect, for much of life's anxiety, fear and trauma, EFT/SET can be healing, especially in the hands of experienced practitioners. This is the 'magic' of energy-point stimulation. Phobias and mild to moderate anxieties respond well to the persistent use of EFT/SET. The key parts of EFT/SET are focus and persistence, so there are advantages to working at length on underlying negative beliefs — if they block progress towards balance.

One definition of brief therapy in the Client-Based Therapy Model of treatment is ten sessions or less, so after completing ten sessions with EFT/SET, a great deal can be achieved with most mild to moderate conditions (and usually less than this number of sessions). These techniques can be invaluable for treating specific incidents, which cause traumatic memories.

But far beyond that are 'severe' conditions, which include moderate to severe clinical depression, psychoses, 'personality disorders' and long-standing addictions. There is also a possibility of a mixture of several conditions that might co-exist with chronic anxiety and chaos. This is where the line might be drawn for many with the usefulness of EFT/SET, because excellent results with conditions such as these are quite rare, if they occur at all.

It is possible that such problems may be 'locked in' to the body–mind in some way outside the reach of many of our current methods of accessing the energy system. They may also have too many powerful aspects for us to achieve 'leverage' using EFT/SET. They may have a strong inner resistance to change that we must work through intensively for months. Or we have not yet discovered a simple way to apply our techniques within the chaotic inner world of many of these people.

Unfortunately, there will probably always be dramas when working with the individual sets of problems that are tagged as 'personality disorders'. No therapeutic approach consistently helps these people in brief therapy according to our definition — and neither does EFT or SET. We think this is because the essential deficiency is thought to be a disorder of the development of the sense of self, due to poor relational experiences as a child. Any successful treatment must therefore be a relational one, and although we have integrated EFT/SET into such treatments (e.g. the treatment approaches of Self Psychology, after Heinz Kohut), we find they don't address that relational issue directly. It takes a lot of time and space, and empathetic attuning with another person, to achieve that relational growth.

Since learning EFT/SET we have completely redefined our approach to any individual and have had some pleasant surprises as a result. Happily, many people do not fit the stereotype of their condition. This particularly applies to treating the physical conditions of those with 'intractable' psychiatric disorders. With

EFT/SET, we often find that both physical and psychiatric conditions show some shift.

'Try it on everything,' as Gary Craig suggests (but here we would add: but don't try it as the sole treatment for serious conditions, especially if you don't know what you're treating!). If you are a therapist with an optimistic approach, realistic expectations and a good amount of training and client experience with EFT/SET, you can frequently offer hope to the hopeless.

# Chapter 6

# Specific Applications of EFT/SET

In this chapter we outline a variety of ways that you can use EFT/SET to improve your life. There is information on using the techniques for both simple and complex issues, including physical ailments and pain, working with children, dealing with severe conditions such as panic, trauma and depression, and using the techniques to help you heal your relationships. We also move beyond the remedial to show you how EFT/SET can be used to heal a negative self-image, assist you to achieve your goals, and help you in your quest for peak performance.

Most of the techniques described in this chapter can be used by ordinary people for self-help, although some issues may be best treated by an experienced practitioner or therapist.

We encourage you to be persistent in treating your personal issues;

sometimes doing EFT/SET at length is a significant factor in gaining a good result, especially with a problem you have had for a long time.

# Using Energy Techniques On Physical Issues

EFT/SET have both shown promise in alleviating a large number of physical issues, including headaches, physical pain, skin conditions, stress-related coughs, asthma, a nervous stomach and most stress-associated conditions. Surprisingly, EFT/SET often help conditions where a result would not be expected — particularly those where orthodox medicine doesn't offer much. This includes, for example, chronic fatigue, coping with disfigurements or irritations and control of prostate or bladder symptoms, in some cases. Very few conditions have proved totally intractable to the effects of EFT/SET.

Gary Craig has recommended with EFT that you 'try it on everything' and we certainly advise you to apply EFT/SET to your physical issues and related symptoms with the proviso that you also have the physical condition checked out by your physician and that you continue with the recommended treatment, using EFT/SET as complementary treatments. Chest and head pain should NEVER be ignored and should be something for which you seek immediate medical advice.

In our experience, all physical conditions have a psychological and emotional component. This is what EFT/SET may most profitably treat — and by doing so, if your emotional state is improved, you will have more energy available to assist the process of physical healing.

Ultimately, the body heals itself. Sometimes what is needed is to get yourself out of the way of the process. If you are very upset about a physical condition, your distress may amplify and even complicate your symptoms. So, in other words, there are two problems here: the original one, and then the emotional one caused by your *reaction* to having that problem. The self-critical elements of the 'second' problem may, over time, emotionally outweigh the first one!

Tapping is an ideal treatment for the second problem, regardless of the cause, because it treats the 'suffering'. Using EFT/SET on the emotions we have associated with the physical problem is a good first step in beginning the healing process. Here's how you can begin, whatever your physical condition:

- Start by identifying any physical sensations associated with your condition. In the case of painful conditions such as headache, this will be easy. In this case, simply focus on the area of pain and conduct rounds of EFT/SET until the pain recedes.

- Expect to achieve some relief of pain or discomfort using EFT/SET and persist until you do so. But realise that you may not be able to achieve total pain relief — usually pain is an important message that there is something wrong and, in the case of a physical condition, this may also require physical treatment, in order for the condition to get totally better.

- Having said the above, however, never assume that the result you have achieved is all that is possible. For example, if your pain that began at a level 9 has receded to a level 6, don't stop there. Always assume that, with persistence, you may be able to achieve more relief — and possibly even the complete end of symptoms. Some people who have been living with painful conditions for many years are extremely pleased to learn that, with a few days of persistent tapping, their conditions can be significantly relieved.

Here are some further guidelines for working on physical issues:

1. Focus on the precise location of the pain: it is better to tap while focusing specifically on your 'right knee pain' than the more general 'pain'. If you have several pain locations, begin by tapping while focusing on the most painful one.

2. Chase the pain: often, when applying EFT/SET, the location and nature of the pain will change. It is important to follow these changes and apply EFT/SET to each 'new' pain location and type. Sometimes the pain may intensify, and if so, keep tapping! Usually a further round or two will make a significant difference to your overall state.

3. Identify emotions to tap on: begin by identifying the emotions you have associated with the problem. What issues does it cause you? Does it frustrate you? Does it cause you to feel weak? What do you fear that it might ultimately lead to? Often tapping on these emotional states can cause changes in your physical experience of the problem. Next, consider what, if anything, may be the emotional cause of the problem. A useful question to ask yourself is: 'If this problem had an emotional cause, what would it be?' You don't have to be certain what caused it at all. Just ask yourself what may have been the emotional cause — or what may be related to it in an emotional sense — and apply the tapping process to that. If you can identify when the problem started, you may be able to identify particular events on which you can apply the tapping process.

4. Persist with EFT/SET on a daily basis: spend some time tapping on the physical symptoms, particularly chronic conditions,

coupled with some time on the emotional issues — or on 'whatever you are worrying about'. It's a good daily prescription, no matter what your physical issue may be.

# Using Energy Techniques with Children

Using Energy Techniques with your own children can be a most rewarding experience. It can also be extremely frustrating. Here are three things we have learned from using EFT/SET with children.

Firstly, you may need to do the tapping on yourself and your own emotions to begin with. If you do some tapping with your child and it isn't working, we suggest this is the first place you should look, particularly with younger children. They tend to be intimately tied to your own emotional state, in that they resonate with your feelings to determine how they are going to feel. Remember, emotions get transferred between people when we interact, and children are often like tuning forks for our emotional states. Here, Steve recounts a story of using the Energy Techniques to help with his eldest son's fear of ghosts.

'One night, some years back, my son Josh, then aged six, was frightened to go into his room alone, telling me he was scared there might be ghosts in there. After explaining that there were no ghosts, and that his light was still on — traditional linear parental logic — he still refused. I told him I would do "the tapping" on this to help him to be less afraid. He replied that the tapping would not work (the Apex Effect is rife even with young children!). I ignored this protest and proceeded to rub on his sore spot and say, "Even though you're scared of ghosts, you're still a good kid." Following several rounds and no reduction in fear I, in my frustration, implemented Plan B: exposure treatment — "Feel the fear and do it anyway kid!"

What followed was a very upset little boy who went to his room under extreme sufferance, which was followed by another performance when going to the bathroom to brush his teeth, and still more crying and upset over going to the toilet. Following this, and with me feeling like a total chump for forcing him to suffer so, I took a moment to think and do some tapping on myself. Then, having produced a little necessary distance, I sat down on the bed with Josh and started to talk about what was scaring him so much.

As I was now no longer anxious about his anxiety (or as frustrated with it), I found I was available to listen to Josh more fully — and target the treatment towards Josh's specific fears — and Josh was surprisingly more receptive to the EFT as well. Josh told me about a segment in a TV program with an airship full of ghosts — not only the images, but also what was said on the program, had upset him. I asked if Josh would be able to focus on that while we did the tapping and he agreed.

As he did so, I was able to realise that the slight distance I now had was crucial to getting this to work for him. I needed to be free of my own negative emotional states ABOUT his problem, in order to work with Josh on his problem. Prior to this my emotions were clouding my reactions — and were even being transferred to him, short-circuiting our work together. (I believe if we anxiously tap with someone or on someone else, we greatly lessen the chances of a positive result — this is why I always tap along with my clients. I don't want my own state to interfere with their healing.)'

The conclusion to this story is that they were then able to proceed through several aspects, with Steve being respectful enough of his son to ask him at each point *'What should we call that?'* when they identified aspects to tap on, involving Josh more fully in the process. Five rounds later and Josh went off to sleep. Problem solved — at least for now!

Our advice to parents, counsellors and therapists is to always tap on yourself. We have experienced numerous situations where this one action has made all the difference.

Secondly, treat yourself for the things your children (and other people) do that upset you. Again, Steve tells a story of dealing with his newborn daughter's crying.

*'When my daughter was born, her particularly loud cry and inbuilt persistence had a significant negative effect on me. I found it stressful to deal with her at these times of auditory assault.*

*One day, while changing her nappy with her screaming and me getting upset, I realised that I needed to do some tapping on this. A few rounds of tapping on "her cry" and I suddenly became aware of the wide variety of different cries she actually produced. Previously they were all the same — loud and intensely upsetting for me. Now I realised that some cries were due to real pain, some were due to frustration, some were simply wanting a little love and affection, and so on. Previously, they all translated to me as intense suffering, and that was painful for me to have to cope with, especially when a particularly tired girl could take up to an hour to settle down to sleep.*

*After tapping on myself over her cry and the effects it was having on me, I was able to realise that not all of her cries required an immediate response, or the same type of response, or even any response on occasions. And I began to feel good about my little girl again. Being able to "stand in the heat" was empowering for a father who never would have been able to cope with this without the tapping. Now, she is able to do the tapping for herself if she can't sleep.'*

Thirdly, make tapping like a game, or into something that you share and take it lightly with your young child. Jo Wiese, co-author (with Steve) of a children's book on EFT titled *Rose and the Night Monsters*, often uses the analogy of EFT as a 'tap dance' that you do with your fingers! Although set-up statements, as used in EFT, are generally not necessary with children, they can have a place. For example, in a natural way, when talking with your child about their worries and fears you can make such simple statements as, 'Even if you're a bit scared, Mummy and Daddy love you.' Then you tap on the points while saying 'scared a bit'. They will usually respond, get involved and used to it, and become comfortable with the technique — which most often you will be doing for them. This ensures that when you need it in a very stressful situation, you have the right framework in place for using EFT/SET effectively. Children tend to respond to tapping more rapidly than adults, and are far more open about their upset feelings.

What follows are some stories from Steve on how tapping has helped his children and the children of others to overcome emotional upsets. We hope you will find them inspiring and also instructive on ways you can help children with tapping.

## OVERCOMING A FEAR OF SANTA CLAUS

One Christmas, the first after I had learned EFT, I was given a strong reminder of the joy we can bring when we use these techniques to help others. I was at a Christmas party organised by my wife's playgroup — a group that, at the time, met on a weekly basis. The previous year, the children had all been about two to three years of age, and meeting Santa was, for many of them, a bit of a challenge — most were overwhelmed, many cried and some wouldn't go near this strange man in the red suit, even after frantic attempts by parents to pacify them.

This particular year, with the kids a year older, the parents fully expected it to be different, since most of the children were looking forward to seeing Santa, now having learned the association between Santa and presents! All except for a little girl I will call Hannah.

As everyone stood waiting for Santa to arrive, Hannah's mother told me how her little girl was frightened to the point of almost hysteria, even by the very *thought* of Santa. In fact, she also had this reaction whenever other children's characters (even friendly ones like teddy bears) were around — she would scream and run away.

With only a little time before Santa arrived, I hastily explained a short version of EFT tapping for anxiety and fear, suggesting she tap on her daughter a few times under the eye, on the collarbone point, and under her arm before Santa arrived and again when he did. As Santa made his way down the path a few minutes later, Hannah became very upset and frightened and ran into her mother's arms. Her mother, with a worried look, started trying desperately to do the tapping, while holding her girl tight.

A minute later, after leaving her daughter sitting on a rug with her husband, Hannah's mother came back to tell me that it 'didn't work', and that her daughter was still very upset. I had been watching her daughter the whole time, however, and so I pointed the mother towards the front of the group, where her husband was now walking with their daughter, holding hands, towards Santa.

We watched as Hannah walked up to Santa with a smile on her face, accepted a gift from him, and even paused for a while to talk to him, smiling happily as she did so. You should have seen the proud, relieved faces on both of her parents.

Postscript: I was later informed that not only did this little girl's fear of Santa and other children's characters improve, but her fear of dogs also went away as a result of that treatment! At the time this incident happened, Hannah's mother could not accept that the tapping had produced the result — the Apex Effect in full flight. However, a few years later she referred a friend to me whose little boy had a phobia of dogs, almost eight years after the incident described here!

## JOSH LEARNS MULTIPLICATION TABLES RAPIDLY

When my eldest son Josh was ten years old, he mentioned over dinner one evening that his teacher was threatening to send him to the lower maths class due to his continuing poor performance in mental maths tests (you remember, those tests you did at the start of maths class where the teacher called out maths problems and you had to solve them in your head and put down the answers). Josh had received just four out of ten on the test that day and had been told that unless he received seven out of ten on the next day's mental maths test, he would be sent down to the lower class. He was very concerned about this because the teacher told him that 'all the lower class does is worksheets all day'.

My wife Louise and I were concerned about the teacher's approach, however, we decided to assist Josh as much as we could. Since the mental maths questions were mainly based on multiplication tables, we decided to see if we could practise those tables with Josh in preparation for the next day's test. The tables Josh didn't know were 6x, 7x, 8x and 9x.

Louise taught Josh a simple process for remembering 9x tables and he seemed to pick this up fairly well. However, he still had all those other tables to learn and the test was the next day. Fortunately for him the teacher was away sick the next day and he had a reprieve! The next night I sat down with Josh to teach him the other tables.

As soon as I sat down with Josh and started to ask him about his tables, I saw him do a big sigh and go into a low-energy state. In this state, he wasn't able to recall any of the tables we were working on and it was clear that this negative state was affecting his performance at school. As I saw him sigh again, I said, *'this is the real problem — that bad feeling you are having'* and asked Josh if he would like to try tapping on it to see if he could feel better about doing his maths tables. Josh was very receptive to EFT/SET since I have used them with him since he was three years old.

As I tapped on the points for him, I was also simultaneously talking with him about his maths and about what he was feeling. Josh said he was worried about going down to the lower class, so we did some tapping on that. (Mostly we were doing continual tapping as we talked about things rather than formal set-ups, although each time Josh came up with another aspect we did an initial set-up on that aspect.) He then went on to tell me that he felt bad about the teacher yelling at him and we did some more tapping on the hurt and scared feelings about that. During the time we were tapping Josh also remembered some other times that the teacher had yelled at him and we did some more tapping for the feelings caused by those incidents. All in all we did about 15–20 minutes of tapping on specific aspects, then some continual tapping as we practised the 6x tables. I was surprised that Josh learned his 6x tables completely in a matter of minutes!

The next day Josh's teacher was still away, however, the relief teacher did a mental maths test with the class. Josh came home to announce proudly that he had achieved 45 out of 50 and told us that he'd been surprised to find that the entire test seemed like it was almost completely based on the 6x tables! I began to think that the Universe was on our side as I congratulated Josh on his success.

That night we did another session of teaching Josh the 7x and 8x tables. Again, we did continual tapping on the points while going through the tables, all the while encouraging Josh to recite and visualise the tables in his head while I tested him. And, again, I was completely amazed that he was able to learn the whole lot in only 20 minutes! This, more than any other experience, taught me that when we are emotionally open and ready to learn we are capable of learning incredibly quickly.

Again, the teacher was away so we were fortunate to have another night to practise the tables with Josh, although now all we were doing was testing him — he no longer needed to program the tables into his mind, just to recall them easily.

The next day Josh came home to announce that the teacher was at school and he had achieved ten out of ten on the mental maths test! Although he knew he was still under threat if he didn't continue to perform, his newfound confidence was clearly evident. The next day Josh achieved eight out of ten on the test and cemented his place in the class.

A few days later Louise was dropping Josh off at school when the teacher happened to mention how pleased and surprised he was about Josh's instant turnaround. During the course of the conversation he mentioned the 'threat' and apologised for it, telling her that he had made it out of frustration and hadn't realised what a strong effect it might have on Josh. Later she and I both met with the teacher and told him that having experienced our own frustrations with Josh at times we could afford to be forgiving on this point. He was relieved, as his intentions had been positive and he'd really just wanted to motivate Josh to improve.

In our meeting, Josh's teacher pointed out that Josh was not only performing better, but that his entire attitude and demeanour in the classroom had changed. This change had also spread into other areas of his schoolwork and his general preparedness and personal organisation had also improved.

Josh continued to improve and a few weeks later he received an honour certificate at the school assembly for 'Instant and significant improvement in mental maths work'. The best thing of all, however, is that he stopped sighing when thinking or talking about mental maths — in fact, for quite a while, he would beam whenever he talked about it!

## OLIVIA OVERCOMES HER DENTAL FEAR

We were advised by an orthodontist that our daughter Olivia (aged seven at the time) would need to have four baby eye teeth removed in order to allow her adult teeth to come through in the correct positions. He suggested she could either have them removed in the chair or under general anaesthetic. As she had coped extremely well when having a cap put on another tooth with a local anaesthetic, we decided to have them removed two at a time this way, by the dentist. In the dentist's room, while the local anaesthetic was starting to take effect, Louise noticed that Olivia was looking a little bit upset and teary so she asked the dentist if she could explain to Olivia what was going to happen to her. At this point Louise could see Olivia was getting more and more upset, so she asked her if she would like her to do some tapping for her. She said yes, so Louise began tapping on her face points and after a few minutes Olivia started to calm down and the tears stopped. Louise then had to explain to the amazed dentist and her assistant what on earth she was doing! Throughout this time Olivia's brother Callum kept asking, 'When is it my turn? I want a turn!'

By this time the anaesthetic had numbed the area and it was time to remove the teeth. Olivia was okay to start, but asked that Louise continue the tapping. Louise stood out of the way of the dentist and tapped on her hand points throughout the procedure. The dentist and assistant were very impressed about Olivia's turnaround so Louise said she would bring back some EFT information on their next visit. On the way home in the car Olivia was very upset; she had managed to control her emotions with the help of the tapping to get through the dental procedure, but was still feeling pretty awful and it now all came out. When they got home Louise realised that, although she had done some tapping on herself in the car on the way home, she was also feeling awful — how could she have let her child go through such a horrible thing? She had felt the need to tap on herself in that dentist office, but was too busy concentrating on Olivia and believed Olivia was picking up on her upset as well. So they all did some more tapping once they got home and were all fine in a little while.

Two weeks later, having to go back to the dentist for the removal of the other two teeth, Olivia had already decided to take her copy of *Rose and the Night Monsters* to show the dentist. I did a little bit of tapping with her before she went, although she was more interested in eating her lunch than having a session with her dad! The dentist and assistant were very impressed with the book and took some EFT cards to show other clients. Olivia sailed through the procedure, not requiring any tapping. Louise knew she was fine when she asked her, 'What's for dinner?' through a mouth full of gauze before they even left the reception area!

## CALLUM'S BLOOD TEST

Our youngest son Callum has Down syndrome. He generally doesn't seem to need a lot of tapping — he lives in the moment, is happy if the PlayStation or Wii is working, or if he can bounce on the trampoline or play with the dog. He also doesn't worry too much about future events, except, 'What are we doing today?' and 'What's for dinner?'

Callum needs to have a battery of annual blood tests to check his thyroid, iron levels and several other concerns common in people with Down syndrome. This blood testing has been challenging at times, as Callum has low muscle tone and chubby little arms (as is common with people with Down syndrome), and it is often quite difficult to find a good vein. One year, they needed to take quite a lot of blood to test his immunity levels for chicken pox, diphtheria and tetanus.

When Callum was nine years old, we went for the annual blood test to the local pathology clinic (Callum remembered the clinic from the last few years and started to let us know his displeasure at being there from the carpark onwards). When we had said he was going for a test, he thought he was going to a cricket test, not a blood test! Callum began calling out, 'I want to go home … I'm all better'. Unfortunately, after two unsuccessful attempts to find a vein we went home.

Louise spoke to several people she knew who had had trouble with collapsing veins and got a few leads for pathology clinics worth trying. She also got suggestions on how to help the blood flow, such as keeping Callum warm, drinking lots of water, and so on. Two weeks later, she went with Callum and Olivia to another pathology clinic where two very experienced phlebotomists work. Callum was not happy at this point, calling out, 'I want to go home', 'I've already had my test', and so on. Louise explained the situation to the ladies and one of them had to leave the room before she even started, as she felt slightly faint with the pressure. Back in the room, with Louise lying on Callum so he couldn't wriggle around and kick, and the other woman holding his arm still, after much poking and prodding with the needle, they managed to locate a vein. Very slowly blood started to come out. Very slowly. Ten vials needed to be filled. Next, the phlebotomist tried a syringe to drag out the blood and then the flow stopped altogether. 'This sometimes happens with kids,' she said. 'You may need to go to the children's hospital. This is an exceptional case,' All the while Callum was saying, 'There is no blood, there is no blood, I'm all better, I want to go home.'

After a little while, they decided to give the other arm a go and tried all the tricks, including placing a glove full of warm water on his arm to try and bring out a vein, yet they still couldn't locate one that didn't disappear as soon as Callum's arm moved even slightly. The nurse eventually managed to find one in his wrist near his thumb. At this stage Callum was sitting up with Louise holding him to keep him still. He was still calling out. The phlebotomist finally found a vein and a small amount of blood appeared. At this point, Louise was feeling like an awful mother, thinking that she was going to have to make Callum go through this all over again at the children's hospital. Callum was still complaining and kept saying, 'There is no blood, the blood's all gone.'

Out of the blue, Olivia, Callum's twin sister who had been sitting quietly in the corner during all this called out, 'Why don't you tap him, Mum?' Of course! She hadn't even thought of that as she had been too busy holding Callum still so he didn't get hurt by the needle.

Louise began to randomly tap on Callum's face and the collarbone point. Amazingly, the blood started to flow and Callum stopped calling out. The blood was flowing so well, in fact, that the phlebotomist filled all the vials and then started to completely fill vials that she previously had just the minimum amount in. She said, incredulously, 'This is amazing!'

Now Callum had fully relaxed. Louise removed her other arm from him and just sat next to him. No more tapping was needed. Much relieved, Louise left behind two exhausted phlebotomists who probably wished to retire before our next visit, and went to the shops to buy some hot chips for a very brave boy and a very clever girl!

# Trauma Self-Help Using EFT/SET

Trauma is emotional upset caused by your being hurt. The cause could be mental, emotional or physical. You experience a traumatic incident, but you also have a reaction to that trauma. This second reaction can be quite major if the event is extreme.

While the serious condition of 'post-traumatic stress' is narrowly defined (involving the fear of being killed or being seriously injured), less violent situations may also affect you very deeply. Ordinary accidents and even life's usual emotional traps and hurdles can cause serious problems if you are a sensitive person. Such problems include anxiety, depression, emotional 'numbing', mental 'flashbacks', intrusive thoughts, mental vigilance (increased arousal), sleep disturbance and any of the physical signs of stress.

### WHAT EXACTLY IS SELF-HELP FOR TRAUMA?

Self-help means that by using healing techniques and ordinary support (friends and family), you overcome your emotional upset through your own efforts. Almost by definition this means minor trauma — the trauma experienced in day-to-day trials or tribulations — and can include very minor car accidents and setbacks at work, for example. Likewise, the symptoms are relatively mild.

It is unwise to try and treat yourself alone for serious reactions, usually to major trauma. This might include reactions to shock (as in the September 11 televised images of destruction), grief, assault and bullying. If you work in the emergency services (fire, police, ambulance), have a regular connection with the armed forces, or have had a series of accidents or illnesses, or any chronic stress or previous serious emotional issues in your life, you might need extra help as a result of having come into contact with very disturbing things. *If you have any doubt — see a professional.*

Some of the 'minor trauma' triggered by your being rejected does not feel minor at all. In relationships, at work, or at school, such emotional repercussions need quite a lot of early and repeated tapping. This is because they remind us of other times and hurts, and violently affect our self-esteem. The role of tapping here is one of 'first aid' and as a coping strategy.

The technique of 'Telling the Story' is ideal. You can also 'Run the Movie' if you are comfortable with making mental images. Both these techniques, which are outlined below, were invented by Gary Craig and are very practical (a full explanation is on his website at www.emofree.com). A short period of specific EFT/SET work could bring better balance to nearly all everyday irritations. Ideally, you do this as soon as possible after the upsetting experience, for the best outcome.

## THE 'TELL THE STORY' TECHNIQUE

This is a technique for treating past events and negative or traumatic experiences using EFT/SET. It basically involves recounting what happened to you and progressively applying the tapping technique to the emotionally intense parts of the memory or experience — as well as any associated negative thoughts or beliefs — until you feel relief and are able to recount the experience from a position of greater calm and balance.

## Step 1

Treat yourself with EFT sequences or SET continual tapping on any concerns or doubts related to doing this treatment, and any connected negative beliefs, if you can identify these.

## Step 2

'Tell the Story' of what happened in your mind (or out loud if you are working with another person), step by step, such that if you feel emotional intensity (upset) at any point, stop the account and treat yourself with EFT sequences for relief. Alternatively, apply SET in the form of continual tapping and control the amount of time you tap when there is intensity. Focus on the strongest impressions, which, for you, could be images, self-talk or body feelings. After gaining reasonable relief, start the account again.

## Step 3

When you have finished, stop and review the story (tell it again). Make sure there is no residual intensity. You should be able to relate the incident with a neutral kind of feeling. Now scan your body for any tension and treat that if present (i.e. focus on it and tap).

## THE 'RUN THE MOVIE' TECHNIQUE

This is very similar to the 'Tell the Story' technique except that, in this case, you make the negative experience into a small movie in your mind and apply tapping to it, as follows:

### Step 1

Treat yourself with EFT sequences or SET continual tapping on any concerns or doubts related to doing this treatment, and any connected negative beliefs if you can identify them.

### Step 2

Make a mental movie of a negative event (which is, by definition, a specific event). If you can't, the problem is too 'global' in your mind and you need to select something more specific to work on. You could focus on the 'first' time, the 'worst' time, or the 'most recent' time it happened. When you have identified an event to work on, start the mental movie and tap, but be sure to stop if there is emotional intensity (upset), and allow extra time for tapping until the intensity reduces. Continual tapping, as used in SET, is ideal here because the images usually don't lend themselves to the interpretation of typical EFT sequences without stopping the whole process.

### Step 3

When you have finished, stop and run the movie through again in full colour and sound, taking about a minute. Make sure there is no residual intensity. Now scan your body for any tension and treat that if present (i.e. focus on it and tap).

For deeper problems, the key to achieving good results is to *focus* and to *persist*. It is better to do a lot of tapping on the hurt feelings, even if you are unsure about the words to say or exactly what the issues are. If so, continual tapping is the ideal thing to use.

Focus either on the mental aspects of the problem (the associated memories, thoughts, ideas, images and sounds) or on the emotional feelings and physical feelings in the body (any tension, aching, or feelings that come up in certain places). Persistence pays. This may mean doing many sequences during the time you set aside (say 30 minutes) and/or doing continual tapping (without a set-up statement) any time you have intense feelings.

You can treat yourself in public by discreetly rubbing or touching the points, or simply holding any of the points, particularly the finger points. You can also use a process called 'Touch and Breathe', developed by Dr John Diepold, which simply involves holding the points and 'breathing into' each one. Just thinking about using EFT/SET will often bring relaxation and benefits.

For severe trauma and more complex issues that do not respond to self-help, consider seeking treatment with an experienced practitioner.

## TREATING SEVERE TRAUMA

Here David tells the story of treating his own daughter after she suffered a severely traumatic experience. When this session was conducted he was still using original EFT, although he was using an almost constant tapping process (it was exactly this kind of trauma treatment session that inspired the discovery of continual tapping). Nowadays, we would use the same basic process, but substitute the continual tapping of SET for formal EFT sequences, as it is our experience that the amount of energy-point stimulation is crucial for the best result. Either lots of EFT sequences or SET continual tapping can produce good outcomes, but continual tapping without using set-up statements often has the edge, because it does not rely on stopping the process in order to construct set-up statements. It is also far more natural and conversational, since you are concentrating only on the issues and not the tapping.

'My daughter Tanya was at the epicentre of the Bali terrorist bombing on 12 October 2002. With her permission I disclose details of her treatment for the trauma of that night. My hope is that many others affected by this kind of disaster will come to use EFT/SET — personally or professionally — as straightforward and effective antidotes to the hurt from experiencing the implicit horror of such events.

The technique is relatively simple. The key to a good result, in my opinion, is focus and persistence. "Focus" means using Gary Craig's technique of "Telling the Story" as outlined above; "persistence" means making sure that many tapping sequences are delivered during the treatment session — at times the tapping is constant.

First there was the 4 a.m. call. "Only slight injuries." She is in shock and far away. I started tapping from that point on — and through the next day of unfolding details, of organising a flight home, of reading the details on the Internet and of contacting family. The confirmed death toll rises from three to 183 in 36 hours. The anxiety and worry at a deep level is far more intense than anything I have experienced before, even though we know she is alive. The next morning, we wait at the airport with hundreds of extremely worried people.

Tanya appears and looks very well for someone who has slept little in days. She is upbeat about being alive but she has seen *terrible things. We share our tears. Then, on the way home, we hear the awful story of the blast. But for two trivial circumstances she would have been killed.*

At this point I wish that we could stop and use EFT for everybody immediately but it isn't the right time. At home I find that she is soon going to be interviewed twice, and friends are coming over. I don't want her to repeat her story without EFT first. Steve is in the house at the time and offers to do EFT with her if I don't feel up to it — but I do. It is reassuring to have him around.

She and her boyfriend James agree to a treatment session together. He has been so concerned about her. He, too, had a telephone call. I ask him to tap along with everything Tanya says and feels and get the benefits that way, and say I will check in with him at the end of the session. (Because he is very inclined to help Tanya, I don't explain EFT fully to him — we just start, and he is a very quick learner.) Tanya already knows the EFT basics.

She is okay about going into the story of the event — there is no fear of that, or any block to doing it. The first thing that happens when we start with the tale is that she connects with the feeling of an extraordinary evil "touching my heart like a spider". We divert to treating this feeling in her chest, and then the stomach (as it "shifts") until it lessens. We go through the moments of the incident, using EFT for any intensity during the recollection. While all of the memories have very intense thoughts, the feeling reactions become more neutral as we go on.

I ask Tanya to tap on her cheek point whenever she pauses to give me feedback, or diverts into an association. Then to use her collarbone point or her little finger point (and others that I like such as the yin/yang combination points on the inner or outer wrist) so that she is tapping continually. We don't analyse what she says —

125

we just tap on it instead, for the whole session, either doing set-up sequences, or the SET "going with the flow" tapping.

On two occasions, when she is distressed and engaged by it, I use the extended EFT sequence, otherwise I use the seven-point shortcut sequence exclusively. Sometimes I use one set-up statement for several rounds of tapping. I concentrate, as usual, on the negative (reported) aspects of what has happened, but here I am sensitive to the fact that the worst is represented fully in the body at one level anyway — EFT in trauma work is a multilevel treatment and often works best in the body without clever words. Hence, lots of tapping is required.

I don't take any ratings for intensity but gauge the effect of EFT by the degree of relaxation, hesitations, voice tone and sighing. We are all completely attuned. I am tapping as actively as anyone during the whole session to help and protect myself.

In the process it becomes clear that Tanya kept it together on the night and didn't panic. There was carnage and chaos. Despite being blown over she was able to join with others and give and receive help. There was more danger in her mind during the phase of getting away when she was nearly run over by many speeding motorbikes. Having escaped to the beach from the destruction, she had to deal with people looking at her black face and body, and the owner of her hotel refusing to let her settle her bill and wash herself. There were the surreal aspects of life continuing uninterrupted half a mile away from the carnage, especially the next day. In Tanya's own words:

"I was tapping the whole time I walked away from the club. As the motorbikes came at me, I was tapping. I don't know if it was a short or long while (I'm thinking about 30–45 minutes to get to the beach) but all that stuff was in my head. Later at the beach talking with people, I was imagining I was tapping. I kept thinking 'I'm doing the best I can'…"

I help her finish all of the tapping for the "story" and double check the result by having her go through it again. The event has a more neutral feeling about it now. The story has a second component where she returned to the site the following day and took pictures of the debris and bodies for her newspaper. The full impact of the horror was clear.

Then we see if she has any residual body tensions — and we tap on those too. This is enough for one session.

Following the session she does her interviews, tells her story to friends and watches the TV news with appropriate sadness and feeling. Of course, EFT will not eliminate the legitimate upset and grief associated with such an event — only the dysfunctional and excessive part. She is coping. James is relaxed.

Tanya and James sleep deeply that night. The next day they both feel "fine" and go swimming. They talk together the whole day. Tanya has no "flashbacks" or intrusive thoughts, or nightmares, and is not upset at a deep level. She is celebrating being alive — and I love to see it!

In the evening we have another session (lasting two hours) to check on the treatment and see what else might be worth treating. Some of the chest emotion has returned. It turns out that now there are more philosophical concerns about what the whole evil effort of terrorism might mean. We discuss this while doing a lot of continual tapping, and we also talk about life and death and war and injury but in a neutral to positive way. James recalls an incident where his life was in danger and we tap on the memory of that. Tanya says it is the love and affection of family and friends that has helped most.

I think she has had good treatment for all the aspects of the event that we could discover. I will keep an eye on her (seven years later *she has had no change in her result — the event is not emotionally charged for her).*

*In the media Australia begins mourning the loss of life of its young people. We have lost proportionately more lives than the USA on September 11, 2001.'*

Postscript: *Tanya was in Paddy's Bar when the first bomb went off inside — 40 people were killed instantly. She had moved to a corner to get away from the loud music of Britney Spears. (I find myself warming to that singer in a brand new way.) And a friend refilled her drink then so that, out of politeness, she didn't leave, but lingered behind the concrete wall in this corner that saved her life from the huge car bomb that went off outside a minute later.*

*These are the random unpredictabilities of survival that I find hard to credit and thus, so disturbing.*

*I was more upset about what happened than I initially realised. The tapping process calmed me significantly. When I saw the photograph of the charred remnants of Paddy's Irish Pub, I had to do a lot more tapping (that image bothers me somewhat to this day). And even more when I watched the TV reports of the great efforts of ordinary people to provide care to the injured in impossible circumstances. I still can't think of Tanya nearly dying as a real event.*

*EFT (and SET) does work to help heal severe trauma. Not all this trauma fits the strict criteria for "post-traumatic stress" but it still hurts very much. Tanya used EFT as "first aid" on the night — this is ideal timing for self-help. The earlier you can treat, the better. The ease of use of SET tapping makes it very accessible as "first aid" at such times. I also think that the more energy-point stimulation you do in a treatment session, the better the result. Simple techniques can treat thoroughly. Take your time using EFT/SET and be optimistic that every sequence of EFT and every minute you spend tapping on the energy points using SET promotes real healing. And remember, media reports are traumatising for onlookers, especially when they are public, so use EFT/SET when watching or reading. The continual tapping of SET is ideal in these situations.*

# Panic Disorder

This is a form of anxiety where you have 'panic attacks' and develop strong fears and concerns about such episodes. An attack means that you might be having, for example, anxious feelings, over-breathing, heart palpitations, dizziness, trembling and fear. The problem is common in young adults (an estimated 2 per cent of the population) and the tendency might be inherited. It can be connected to other fears or underlying depression. As a result of having a panic attack, it is very common to form false beliefs. For example, you might believe:

'I am going mad.'

'I could die.'

'I am not in control.'

You also become very concerned about having another panic attack.

## TREATING PANIC DISORDER
The good news is that a panic disorder can be quickly treated so well that you no longer have attacks. The reality is that your system is very

sensitive to life events, stress and negative thoughts. It is so easily 'tuned in' to a state of high nervous arousal. Many things stimulate that nervous system and only a few things settle it down. You must learn how to de-tune your system to first achieve 'emotional fitness' — and then to maintain it. EFT/SET are ideal for this.

Continual tapping in SET should quickly bring you to a state of balance in a few days or weeks if you use commonsense stress management as part of an overall management program. The main benefit of continual tapping is to promote the relaxation response in your body, and that tells your mind that things are okay.

Continual tapping is the antidote if you ever feel anxiety building. It also helps you to prevent further attacks by maintaining your 'emotional fitness'. While the *tendency* to have this disorder may remain, it is unlikely to be a problem afterwards, if treated and maintained correctly.

Of course, it is also vital to deal with your negative beliefs. The three beliefs listed above are caused by the bad feelings during any major attack, and are *not true* (it just feels that way after the intense experience of having an attack). You might also have a *self-critical* reaction: 'I should have been over this a long time ago (and should never have developed it in the first place!)' This is a natural self-criticism for not being able to get over something in a few weeks, or by using willpower. All these beliefs respond very well to the application of tapping since they lose their 'heat' over time. You just tap whenever your beliefs bring on negative thoughts in your mind ('grafting continual tapping on to the problem'). This is the easiest way to interrupt the pattern of your problem.

In the beginning we also suggest you get an assessment from a professional, and do a thorough job of addressing your 'triggers' to this condition.

# Treating Compulsive Disorders and Bulimia

Acceptance tapping is a powerful EFT/SET treatment variation for severe compulsive disorders and bulimia. It is a simple method of starting treatment for many conditions — especially the 'difficult ones'. It follows the work of the famous American family therapist Milton H. Erickson by 'pacing' the experience of the client with a problem, and so meeting them in their view of the world; the techniques of Buddhist awareness; and the 'focusing' work of Eugene Gendlin (we are also indebted to David Hall of Sydney, a mind–body practitioner, for his useful suggestions). It paves the way for acceptance of the reality of the problem, and validation — even if this is validation of the negative. You can stop 'fighting' the problem. This is often the 'missing link' for sufferers when progress is blocked. And it can produce surprising results.

The basic principle is to pay attention to, and work with, what is present, instead of trying to change it.

If you try to change a problem of this nature, it often comes back. Instead, let it be what it is — in essence, you accept that the problem is real before anything else is changed. Then you simply add 'continual tapping' into the problem pattern. We have come to call this process 'acceptance tapping'.

Paradoxically, we found that if, as therapists, we made direct suggestions to the client about change in the beginning, these would usually fail. Possibly these suggestions are too difficult to achieve logically and rationally. In this treatment variation you tend to sidestep the thinking mind — and just tap. You work with the problem using energy meridian stimulation simply as an added pattern to the way the problem presents. This 'interrupts' the problem's own pattern.

It can work with all common behaviours that you don't feel in control of (the treatment of compulsive disorders and bulimia, for example). Any time you tap while the negative feelings are intense, it can be disproportionately helpful. The process can be taught easily and quickly and most of our clients find that part straightforward, gaining the relaxation of EFT/SET initially, when usually there would be the massive stress of anticipating or experiencing the problem.

You may also find that if you do this you will feel less shame about having the problem. There is increased self-awareness instead of the usual automatic reactions when 'triggered'. For example, one girl, while tapping, was able to 'observe herself' getting ready for a vomiting episode, and found that for once she could think about doing it, and *also not doing it* (before tapping, the habit was unstoppable), although she did actually do it at that time. The difference now involved being able to think more clearly. Her 'triggers' for the frustration and anxiety were still there — mainly about feeling 'fat' — but now she could begin to see both sides of the issue more calmly: the reality ('I weigh 60 kilograms'), and the hallucination ('I am fat'). This is potentially very useful.

Continual tapping is a marvellous support for any formal treatment approach.

## SELF-HELP STRATEGY FOR BULIMIA USING SET

The treatment for bulimia is best managed by a professional. The self-help strategy outlined below should form part of a treatment program and should only be seen as a supportive technique. The steps used in this strategy are:

### Step 1

Let things stay exactly as they are now and do continual tapping (one-handed) whenever you feel in the grip of your problem. This means 'experimenting' with using the tapping to 'see what happens' while you have those feelings around eating too much or having to vomit. Maybe you have 'triggers' which set you off? No judging — just tap during the episode, and until the episode is over.

## Step 2

Do plenty of continual tapping in your day to help manage the underlying tensions you feel. This is essential work to build up inner strength.

## Step 3

Rehearse an 'episode' in your mind when it's a good time for you. Use the tapping all the time as you imagine what will happen; either it is a typical episode, or maybe you can imagine a different experience? How do you imagine it will feel for you when you have recovered from this problem? This is using your mind in a healthy way for encouragement. Either you are weakening the pattern of the problem or you are wondering about a more positive future.

## SELF-HELP STRATEGY FOR OBSESSIVE COMPULSIVE DISORDER USING SET

'Diane' was a young woman aged 30 who came to see David because she wanted to become pregnant — but not while taking prescribed antidepressants. She thus wanted to be drug-free and cope with her obsessive compulsive disorder (OCD) using other methods. She had been taking medication for a decade, and had never been able to relinquish it before because of her severe anxieties, and was under the care of a treating psychiatrist. She had good support and was highly motivated. David asked her to see her therapist for the relational aspects of the reassurance she needed during treatment, while he attended to teaching her EFT/SET.

David considered her request a tall order because of the severity of the condition, his limited success with severe OCD using Energy Techniques, and the potential complications for her. Nevertheless, he thought that teaching, and her using, meridian stimulation would be worthwhile. He did not know whether Diane would be able to cease medication at all — and he told her this. He also notified her psychiatrist that he was teaching her a relaxation and stress-management technique that possibly could provide more help in some cases.

Her symptoms included severe compulsive 'checking' of details about the house when going out, and re-checking in most instances as she 'forgot' whether she had really been certain of a detail. The process often took two hours. She also suffered panic attacks and generalised anxiety. She had recently developed a fear of flying and was due to fly shortly. David told her that they would make an experiment and see how much benefit it would be to her.

Initially David taught her continual tapping with good results. She noticed a great lessening of her compulsive urges and was particularly pleased to know a self-help technique. After a week, she found that she was generally much calmer and that the tapping somehow interrupted her obsessive thinking to a degree, but most significantly she was able to leave the house after some 60 minutes at the end of that week. Her re-checking stopped too. This change was effortless for her and quite surprising. She maintained these changes by using the technique a lot, and was able to leave the house in 10–15 minutes after three weeks of treatment.

They began to explore the limiting beliefs she had developed as a result of years of having OCD using EFT/SET and also using the Provocative Style (part of PET: Provocative Energy Techniques — see our website www.eftdownunder.com) that we have found brings great focus and leverage to a problem. For example, some of her greatest fears were that she would never get over this and that she would have it forever, that there was nothing she could do about it, and that it could get worse. Sometimes the fear during an anxiety attack was 'paralysing' and 'terrifying' and Diane's ultimate fear was that 'I can't be reassured'. There were several such intense panic incidents that needed a lot of work to desensitise with tapping, using the 'Tell The Story' technique (see page 120).

Diane continued her practice at home mainly using continual tapping for convenience. She used the tapping David taught her more often and more effectively than anyone he could remember. At the end of the third session she told David that she had ceased her medication since she felt so well using EFT/SET! David was alarmed, since these medications should be ceased gradually, but because she seemed well they pressed on. She also told David that her fear had once returned but it was manageable. She was scared but the fear did subside with the tapping after half an hour. This was a revelation to her and to David. Her fear of flying was '95 per cent gone' because of the EFT/SET treatment.

On another occasion, about six weeks into the treatment, she had a panic and anxiety attack lasting many hours, which did not respond so well to EFT/SET. This was a setback but, nevertheless, they continued the experiment. There was another episode like this a few weeks later.

Diane remained in control of her symptoms thereafter, using EFT/SET, and had what we would call ordinary anxieties about becoming pregnant and being a good mother. Her confidence increased and she functioned with a better balance, becoming more accepting and less self-critical. Her old checking habits and anxieties were still there in a minor way, but did not interfere with her life.

We had some three months of EFT/SET over six sessions, and she became pregnant about six months later. During the later stage of her pregnancy she went to see David about an anxiety she 'couldn't shake', related to whether her worrying would harm the baby and if the baby was, in fact, all right. David dealt with the new fears in the same way as all her original fears and presenting worries — a lot of continual tapping and traditional EFT on every specific aspect he could think of. There was also the fear of the 'unknown', of looking after a dependent baby, and whether she would cope with the responsibilities.

Considering how universal these fears are in mothers-to-be, David was struck by how 'normal' their degree was for Diane. She did not lose control and she did face up to the reality very well, learning more coping skills and just understanding how other people cope too.

Diane's progress from the beginning was very surprising to David. He had not had this kind of rapid success before in such a severe case of OCD, and with relatively few sessions. Because EFT/SET must have had a lot to do with her new balance, the practice of continual tapping at home and while 'in trouble' or while doing one of the compulsive rituals ('acceptance tapping') would have contributed many hours of help. It could not be more simple. Diane certainly found it so. Her main block was 'the fear of the fear' and a degree of helplessness when feeling anxious. EFT/SET eliminated most of this block and she could hold on to reassurance as well as most people, despite everything.

# Energy Techniques and Depression

Depression is a 'low mood' disorder and very common in mild degrees. This is the 'little "d"' which most of us experience at some time in our life. Feelings of hopelessness and negative, dark thoughts make up the depressive thinking that goes with it. Usually it is a reaction to a difficulty, and the low mood soon gets better by itself. The 'big "D"' is clinical depression, and is much worse because it has all these features but much more severely. It can really interfere with normal living. Certainly it removes the fun from life. It needs proper recognition and treatment.

A great difficulty in more severe forms of depression is that your thinking is not working properly (you experience black thoughts, poor concentration, negative beliefs), so your ideas about how to get better are often not helpful to you. Keep in mind that you might respond well to Energy Techniques regardless of the level of depression you suffer, so they are always worth using.

Mild depression usually responds well to EFT/SET. Part of this treatment would, of course, include using exercise, stress management and commonsense. Unfortunately, one area of depression — *moderate to severe clinical depression* — does not respond so well to EFT/SET. This kind of depression is particularly vicious — it is both severe in its effects and consequences. We have not found that the Energy Techniques affect it sufficiently in most cases. Occasionally moderate to severe depression will lift after a short treatment, but this is rare. If any natural method exists that does treat this level of depression reliably and effectively, we have not found it. Some say that specialised acupuncture can achieve this in individuals. There are also reports of individual serious cases of depression responding to the intense personal support offered by some clinics for addiction and dependence.

We have found that unless the depression lifts permanently, you cannot get any meaningful progress. *First you must treat the depression effectively* before using EFT/SET, or any method useful as self-help or therapy, in a relational context. This for us is the path to recovery as things stand today. In the future we hope to have better methods.

## THE ROLE OF MEDICATION

The prevailing popular belief about antidepressant medication today is that it is harmful. In treating serious depression, our opinion is that the right medication can be life-saving, and marriage- and family-saving too. The fact that antidepressants are over-prescribed in some countries to the wrong people for the wrong reasons irritates us, because it can be so helpful to those who really need it. Many people who want to use a natural approach will take the herb St John's Wort readily, and refuse a modern antidepressant. We think there is a huge gap between the idea of treatment and the reality of results for natural treatments of depression. Natural treatments are good for mild depression. Unfortunately, most problems with depression occur when it is more severe. Moderate to severe clinical depression requires a more powerful treatment, ideally a combination of a modern antidepressant (to correct the biochemical imbalance), good self-help methods such as EFT/SET (to facilitate energy balance), and some personal therapy (to help with the depressive thinking). The best multilevel approach would also include an exercise program and dietary changes. This is, in fact, the ideal area for mainstream and alternative medicine to work hand in hand, using a combined approach for best results.

One of the driving beliefs a depressed person typically has is that 'I should be able to get over this myself.' Then there is the medical equivalent of this rigid thinking in the mere prescription of medication, when so much of depression needs intense support and behaviour modification. Even when medication is used, there is still the depressive thinking and beliefs to deal with. Of course, this is where EFT/SET and counselling shine. But first, treat the depression properly if necessary.

To know whether you are suffering from clinical depression, consider these questions:

- Is it severe for you? Has it caused problems for your relationship, family, work?

- Have you tried and failed to 'get over it'?

- Do you think it is just 'stress' or 'all in the mind'?

- Has the depression been around for a long time (many months or more)?

- Do you think you have to get better by yourself, especially without using medication? Is it a shameful thing for you to have? A weakness?

- Have you been like this before in your life?

- Are you using alcohol or drugs a lot (these might be your 'medication')?

- Is there a history in your own family of depression or stress problems?

If the answer to any of these questions is 'Yes', we suggest you have an assessment with a doctor or psychologist, because then you will know the level of your problem and can plan a treatment accordingly. It is so important to find this out that we would not recommend using self-help until you know where you are heading. Then you can use EFT/SET in good faith with a realistic expectation.

If your feelings of depression are mild, short-term, or uncommon for you, and are not causing you major problems, then you can confidently use EFT/SET to help yourself. We would still suggest that you get extra help and emotional support.

## Using EFT/SET for Your Biggest Problem

What is the biggest problem you have? And for each of the problems you have (and most of us have quite a few), what is the biggest problem that having that problem causes you?

We contend that the biggest problem any of your problems cause you is *how they make you feel.*

Think about it. Perhaps you don't like presenting in public. Why? Because it 'makes you' feel anxious. Maybe you don't like boat rides. Why? Because they 'make you' feel woozy. Or you don't like certain people at work because they 'make you' feel annoyed. And because you tend to feel in these ways in these situations, you tend to behave in certain ways — the most common of which is avoidance. How your problems cause you to feel therefore hugely influences your behaviours and therefore your outcomes in life.

If speaking in public causes you to feel excited, if boat rides cause you to feel exhilarated, if interactions with that person in the office cause you to feel powerful, then everything would be different, wouldn't it? The problem would not even be a problem.

If you *felt* differently then you would *act* differently and then everything would *be* different.

So, here you have your problem. Then you have the way(s) the problem makes you feel. And it's *treating these feelings* where EFT/SET come in.

When you want to treat a problem with EFT/SET start by asking yourself:

'How do I *feel* about this problem?' OR

'How does having this problem make me *feel?*'

Then ask repeatedly for every answer you get:

'And how does that make me feel?'

'And how does that make me feel?'

And do some EFT/SET on the answers.

'Even though (this problem) makes me feel X …' or simply, 'This problem makes me feel X' or even more simply 'This feeling' OR

'Even though I feel X about/because of (this problem) …', or simply 'I feel X about/because of this problem.'

Addressing the feeling associated with the problem often takes us towards the most important part of the problem.

To take this further, use the following questions to identify the core events where you learned those feeling associations:

'What does this (feeling) remind me of?' OR

'When/where have I felt this feeling before?'

Search for memories in your past where you had this same feeling and apply EFT/SET to them using the 'Tell the Story' or 'Run the Movie' techniques outlined on pages 120 and 122.

Now let's take this a little further ...

We have come to believe that, ultimately, perhaps the biggest issue our problems cause us is how they make us feel *about ourselves*. Every day people are taking drugs, eating too much, diverting themselves from productive work by watching hours of mind-numbing television or Internet surfing, or doing myriad things because they quite simply don't like the way they feel about themselves. The problems in their life become *the reason* for their own non-self-acceptance. Non-acceptance of self may also be a key part of the cause.

When you solve this problem then all of your other problems may not have gone away but YOU will be different. And when YOU are different, then everything is different.

To continue your progress, ask yourself the following questions:

**'How do I feel about myself for having this problem?'**

**'What does having this problem mean about me?'**

Then do tapping while focusing on these feelings and associations.

To help you, here are some connections that people typically come up with. If you're still breathing it's almost certain you'll have some or all of them:

**'I am angry at myself for having this problem — and for whatever I did to contribute to it.'**

**'I judge myself for having this problem ...'**

**'I am annoyed at myself for having this problem ...'**

'I am upset at myself for having this problem ...'

Having this problem usually means (according to your internal judgement system) that you are a bad person in some way, and the standard statement to describe these associations goes as follows:

'Because I have (this problem) it means I am a bad X (bad X = bad mother, bad father, bad sister, bad brother, bad business person, bad money manager etc) ... '

Insert the appropriate label for yourself and treat yourself for being a 'bad X':

'(Having this problem) means I am a bad X ...'

And treat yourself for the non-acceptance of self that results from having the problem.

If you are using EFT, consider using the following set-up statement at this point (or conduct SET tapping while focusing on it):

'Even though I don't accept myself for having this problem, or for allowing this problem into my life, I fully and completely accept myself.'

Despite the apparent paradoxical nature of this statement, it is one of the truest ones you can make.

When you do this tapping on your non-acceptance, you will often find that it is like unwrapping the layers encasing your problems, and subsequent tapping on the problem itself will yield more dividends, even with problems that have previously resisted treatment. We tell our clients that anger at yourself for having the problem (which almost everyone has to some degree) is like putting a lid on the problem and tends to hold it more strongly to you. Once you treat self-anger, then you can often access the underlying problem and treat it more directly.

Of course, there's another more distressing level to our non-self-acceptance and that is that there are parts of ourselves which *seem to want the problem to exist!* This is your dark side, the side of yourself that you wish didn't exist, that part of yourself which you will do the most to avoid acknowledging, let alone connecting with. That's because we fear that this part will rule us; that if we acknowledge it or even think about it, that it will take us over and then our world will be hell on earth. This is the part that we most enjoy working with, and it's working with this part that has yielded by far the most dividends in our work with clients and participants in our self-acceptance workshops.

As illogical as it seems, accepting your dark side does not empower it at all; not accepting it does! Trying to shy away from it or trying to ignore it often causes it to rise up and bite you. (Our fears tend to come upon us. What we resist persists!) That's because avoiding it, at best, leaves the emotional connection intact and, at worst, reinforces or even increases it.

The ultimate solution is not, as many pop psychology gurus would suggest, to just 'focus on the positive'; the ultimate power comes from being able to think a previously dark thought and realise that it no longer has any power over you.

Shining the light of your awareness — *combined with tapping* — onto your dark side causes it to fade away, and leads you to realise that it really does have absolutely no power — its power exists only because of a mental–emotional construct you formed at one time in your life. The reality is, in fact, a non-reality, the truth a lie, the impact borne only by the strength of the feeling you had associated towards this side, something that EFT/SET and good therapy can transform.

# Self-acceptance

Sometimes it seems impossible to accept yourself just as you are. How can you possibly be happy with yourself when you do such stupid things at times? We tend to resist accepting our problems and 'the way we are' because we believe that if we accept ourselves being and behaving this way, then we will stay this way forever and never change. But this is really the opposite of what happens.

Acceptance of your problem and your current position may be the first essential step before real change can occur. Denial or resistance actually makes for even bigger problems.

By fighting or denying your problems or issues you can actually make them stronger (what you resist persists). You now have a new problem to add to your previous one — the problem of your non-acceptance. This non-acceptance typically manifests itself as self-anger or blame, or as outright denial — and denial requires a lot of psychic energy to maintain. Energy must be used to delude yourself, or distract yourself, or to pretend that the problem isn't real or that it didn't happen, or that you are not like that, or to keep your focus on 'the bright side'. Then you never end up treating the problem, but it sits there in your system, ready to be re-activated anytime you are provoked by life to 'tune into' the bad feelings or bad memories, or when you become 'overloaded by life' and life problems and their accumulated stress causes your problem to rise up in all its former glory. Even worse, however, untreated problems or issues may sit below the surface and ultimately contribute to immune suppression, ill health, and other physical challenges.

The first step to change is to acknowledge your problems. Accept that this problem exists, even though you don't want it to. Yes, it shouldn't be there, yes it's a problem, yes it's frustrating, but its reality is not in question. Once you say yes to a problem, then you can be free to deal with it, to treat it, and ultimately to let it go. But while you continue to say no to it, then it continues to have a grip on you.

Everything you believe (the 'is' of your existence) is ultimately just what you have become attached to. When you release these attachments, you are free to create other beliefs and attachments should you so desire. But isn't ultimate freedom the freedom from having to create attachments at all? Doesn't ultimate freedom exist beyond the pain–pleasure continuum of emotional attachments, of stimulus–response conditioning?

Perhaps we can only release attachments if we realise we have them in the first place. This is one place where we love the set-up statement in EFT — when you are dealing with self-acceptance as *the* issue you are treating. 'Even though I have this problem I accept myself.' The acknowledgement of the problem's existence, and the acceptance of it, is the first part of the statement. Then the acceptance of you is the second part. So the set-up statement actually contains two statements of acceptance: one of accepting the problem (its existence, at least, and maybe its effects); and the other of accepting yourself (the one having the problem). Well, you may not initially accept yourself at all, really; more likely you are upset at yourself, upset at the world, and upset at everything because of the fact that you have the problem. Okay, for the sake of the argument and for now, you are at least going to make the statement 'I accept myself' even though part of you doesn't accept you at all. Rest assured that the part of you that knows you have the problem will feel validated at this point!

This first acceptance, the acceptance of the existence of the problem, is crucial to moving beyond the problem and letting it go, even if all you are *really* accepting is that you can't stand having the problem, that you want to be rid of the problem, that you don't accept yourself for having this problem, that you hate the fact that you don't accept yourself or the problem. How, after all, can you let go of something that you never had? So why not accept that you have it so that you can treat it and then maybe, just maybe, you can take an 'is' and make it a 'was'.

## STEVE'S JOURNEY TO SELF-ACCEPTANCE

A few years ago, Steve set out on a 30-day 'Self-Acceptance Trial'. During this trial he decided to target his own issues of non-acceptance of self as the primary problem — and apply EFT to this. The results have been astounding. In fact, so beneficial were the results that he decided to continue the program indefinitely.

In this section, we'll summarise the process he went through and some of the gains he made, and encourage you to start your own 30-day (or lifelong) self-acceptance trial. We'll also discuss some of the distinctions we have made on the issue of self-acceptance and how this can be addressed in counselling, if required. Here, Steve tells the story of how he achieved greater self-acceptance.

*'For many years I suffered through various problems without realising that underneath them all lurked a bigger problem — I didn't accept myself. Whenever I had a problem, I would be down on myself about the fact that I had it. Or what I was or wasn't doing to fix it. Or I'd just be upset at myself in general, for not measuring up. Now that I have been freed of much of the weight and pressure of this problem, I realise just how pervasive it was, and how insidious its effects were on my energy, performance and enjoyment of life.*

*I also noticed that a lot of my clients were having trouble with self-acceptance too. Usually this came to light when I asked them to make the set-up statement in EFT ('Even though I have this problem I deeply and completely accept myself'). Many clients would become upset and refuse to say the self-accepting part of the statement. How could they say they accept themselves when they very clearly did not?*

*I have faced this issue many times in the past and my usual approach is to have my clients emphasise the negative part of their self-belief and tie that in with a self-accepting statement anyway. For example: 'Even though I don't accept myself (because of this problem), I fully and completely accept myself!' 'Even though I'm a terrible person (and this problem proves it), I fully and completely accept myself!' Many clients are able to move on at this point, and successfully address the problem in question. There is something very powerful in acknowledging the negative parts of self and bringing them into the light, and I have explored this in depth in our workshops and in therapy. In fact, I've found great value in exaggerating the negative aspects even further — an approach David and I call Provocative Energy Techniques (PET — see our website www.eftdownunder.com).*

*For these clients I realised that the underlying issue of non-self-acceptance was THE problem for them, while the presenting problem was just a medium through which this was being expressed. In therapy, I asked these clients to list all the things they didn't like about themselves and applied EFT to these, beginning with the most intense items. I also had them review early parts of their life where they learned that they weren't acceptable, and we applied EFT to these negative emotional experiences.*

*It was at this time that I was going through a period where I wasn't really accepting myself. Basically, I felt I had stalled and wanted to move forward in my work and life but seemed to be making little progress. Instead of doing the things I knew I needed, even wanted, to do, I was wasting many hours playing computer games. This was causing neck and shoulder tension, leading to headaches, which affected my performance and quality of life. I had stalled in my exercise program, my business wasn't moving forward in the ways I knew it could, and I felt like a terrible father to my children, not able to give them the attention they deserved. And I felt terrible about myself. Funnily enough, although my life was actually going pretty well, I felt miserable.*

*One night I found myself sitting frustrated in front of the computer, having played too many games of chess, and feeling really down on myself. In my frustrated state I began typing. As I did this I decided I needed to work on my own issues of self-acceptance right then and there.*

*My first decision was to apply EFT to all of those things I didn't accept about myself. I began to list them and apply EFT to them, just as I had advised my clients to do. I then decided:*

"For the next 30 days, I am going to practise being happy with myself the way I am, despite my limitations, and see what happens ... Each time I find myself doing something I know I 'shouldn't' be doing, I am going to say 'I accept myself even though I am doing X' and conduct EFT on 'Doing X' and on associated thoughts, such as 'Doing X makes me inadequate, bad, awful, etc'."

*Examples of my set-up statements included:*

"Even though I played chess on the computer tonight and that has stuffed up my neck, shoulders, jaw and back for another evening, I fully and completely accept myself."

"Even though I am a bad person for playing chess when I should have been working, I fully and completely accept myself."

"Even though I am never going to be successful if I keep taking myself backwards like this, I fully and completely accept myself."

*I followed the thread of my thoughts as other underlying, irrational and related negative self-defeating beliefs came up, and then proceeded to tap on these. For example:*

"Even though I am probably not going to keep this (30-day trial) up, I fully and completely accept myself."

"Even though I will just have another mediocre year and not achieve real, lasting success, wealth, happiness and joy, I fully and completely accept myself."

"Even though I will end up losing my family if I become too successful, I fully and completely accept myself."

*As I did EFT on these irrational thoughts I noticed my thinking was actually becoming more and more rational — it was not a case of denying problems but, instead, being empowered to address them head on.*

*I continued, addressing other negative and limiting beliefs that have blocked my success, including beliefs about confidence ("I'm not confident enough"), spirituality ("If I become really successful I might lose my soul"), money and self-worth ("How much I charge is a reflection of my self-worth", "I can't charge more because I'm not worth it") …*

*I realised it wasn't the truth of these beliefs that was the problem, but the intensity they provoked in me. Some beliefs still registered as true even after tapping, however, what had changed was that I no longer evaluated myself negatively for them. Instead, I understood how I had come to be that way, and had an increased sense that this could and would change. I wouldn't say I became determined in the sense of willpower, it was more a knowing that it is okay the way it has been, okay the way it is AND it will be okay for me to change things.*

*I found the same for several other emotionally laden thoughts that had been bugging me for many months.*

*Another interesting experience during this experiment was that, in most cases, when I tapped on the fact that I was putting things off or doing things other than what I "should" be doing, I became more willing and able to do the things I had been putting off. Hmmm. This could be the cure for procrastination — self-acceptance!*

*Despite my initial success, however, I still had an underlying sense of inadequacy that I couldn't seem to shake. Then I made one change in my approach that led me to a major breakthrough ...*

## The Breakthrough

*For 30 days I had committed myself to tapping on "Accepting myself despite my limitations". I'd had some initial success, but on day five I achieved a breakthrough ...*

*I was sitting in front of my computer that evening reviewing the notes I had made. I realised that, despite some success, I was still feeling down on myself and didn't seem to be getting far enough just applying EFT to the presenting issues and related beliefs. I needed to address the issue of self-acceptance more directly. I typed the following:*

## "I FULLY AND COMPLETELY ACCEPT MYSELF."

As I considered what associations I had to the idea of accepting myself, I realised that the truth was that I didn't accept myself at all. I decided this was the issue that needed to be met head-on, not all those things I'd been amassing as reasons not to accept myself.

As I began tapping, I realised that underlying my non-self-acceptance was a fear that accepting myself was bad and would lead me down the path of ego. I also believed that if I accepted myself for all the things I had been doing that were wrong then I might not fix them. I might just continue to procrastinate and do things that weren't really good for me. At a deeper level I also believed I was unacceptable to God.

So I tapped on these beliefs in both positive and negative form. I applied EFT to each negative belief by putting it into the set-up statement and repeating the full statement at every tapping point. As I tapped on each statement, I paid attention to the thoughts and feelings that came up with it and applied EFT to any negative and related beliefs that were elicited. For example:

"Even though if I accept myself completely I won't keep improving, I fully and completely accept myself."

"Even if I fully and completely accept myself, I am still a good person."

Underneath, I believed I would not be a good person if I accepted myself. This was connected to some deeply held spiritual beliefs from my early (negative) religious programming, so I tapped on:

**"Even though I fully and completely accept myself, I am still acceptable to God."**

*This caused a very negative reaction. I thought: "No I am not fully and completely acceptable to God! God wants me to be better and to do better ..."*

*So I tapped on: "Even though God couldn't possibly accept me the way I am, I fully and completely accept myself" and "Even though I am completely unacceptable to God, I fully and completely accept myself."*

*I then began to think: "This (non-self-acceptance) is rubbish! Jesus forgave people their sins. Do I think God will not accept me? Forgive me? Aren't acceptance and forgiveness just two sides of the same coin?"*

*I continued to explore my underlying fears. It seemed to me that too much self-acceptance could lead to me being ego-driven and making out that I was superior, like a god.*

*I applied EFT to this by putting it into the set-up statement and repeating it at every tapping point just as I had done with the previous belief statements ("Even if I accept myself completely I will be unacceptable to God ..." and "Even if I accept myself I'm making out that I'm superior ...")*

*I then thought: "Rubbish! I'm not making myself God by accepting myself. I'm merely revelling in what He has created. Shouldn't I love myself AND my neighbour AS myself? How can I love my neighbour as myself if I don't love myself?"*

*Finally, after several more rounds of tapping, I had an intense realisation: "Accepting myself is NOT the same as ego taking over. God loves and accepts me unconditionally, I just haven't accepted myself. Accepting myself IS good."*

And then a whole host of positive thoughts and feelings came rushing in. It was as if all the things I wanted to believe and knew were really true finally felt true. I felt I re-connected with my true purpose and all the barriers just melted away.

As these positive thoughts flooded my being, they were accompanied by a feeling of peace that is difficult to describe, a feeling that lasted several days and bathed me in its light.

For the first time I realised the true power of self-acceptance, and saw the stupidity of our prevailing belief that we need to put ourselves down in order to get ourselves to do things to make ourselves happy. I realised I could be happy no matter what I did, and no matter what was happening around me — and that this would not impede me from moving forward; it would actually help me to do so. I also realised being happy with myself meant I could do so much more for others ...

From this point onwards I was able to effortlessly proceed with my work, attacking with relish projects in which I'd been bogged down for months. I didn't even feel like doing the things I had previously been doing that were distractions. I no longer found myself playing games on the computer. I was able to reinstate my exercise program and improve on it. I started to enjoy my work again and felt I was back to working 'on-purpose'. To put it simply, my life changed, and so did the lives of others with whom I began to share these insights.

Now whenever problems come up, besides addressing the problem itself, I also address the issue of self-acceptance. I encourage you to do the same. I've found that whenever I confront a problem I'm now able to see it as separate from myself, and even when something I am doing is a problem I don't usually get down on myself about it, I just focus on the best way forward.

*I believe the issue of self-acceptance, an issue that has been staring us in the face every time we do the set-up statement in EFT, offers a doorway to a new level of being in the world, and a new level of self-growth and happiness.*

*If you'd like to see how far self-acceptance tapping can take you, here are the first two steps I recommend you take:*

- Identify any problem to work on using EFT/SET. Apply EFT/SET to the idea of accepting yourself, despite having this problem (and even if you continue to have this problem). Repeat the self-acceptance statement at each tapping point in the same form as you used it in the EFT set-up (i.e. "Even though I have this problem I fully and completely accept myself"), and state it as you tap on each point. Meditate on the idea of accepting yourself — as unacceptable as this may feel — while you tap on each point.

- Catch yourself in non-acceptance, then do EFT/SET on the very thing(s) that you are not accepting yourself for. Now focus on two different ideas: one that you accept yourself, despite the fact that you are doing or thinking this thing, and two that, even though you do not accept yourself for doing or thinking this thing, you are going to accept yourself anyway, even though what you are doing or thinking is unacceptable … this treats you for the second wounding — that of picking on yourself for picking on yourself. When you have treated the upset at yourself for your problem then you are free to address the original problem … and sometimes this feeling about the problem is the main issue. Once this is treated, often no trace of the original problem remains.

### Going Further

*After my initial breakthroughs on self-acceptance I was interested to explore whether there were additional insights and freedoms to be attained.*

*Around this time I read a post by Patricia Carrington entitled* Self Acceptance Without Judgment, *which detailed her findings in adjusting the self-accepting statement to include the phrase "without judgment". I tried this and found it quite useful, and felt that it definitely added another dimension to the personal work I was doing.*

*Each day I also receive several inspiring quotes in my email inbox from various sources, and one day the following Chinese proverb arrived:*

**"Deal with the faults of others as gently as your own."**

*When I read this I thought "Wow, I don't deal with my faults gently at all!" So I tapped on …*

**"Even though I am tough on myself …"**

**"Even though I won't allow myself to have faults or make mistakes …"**

*I followed my thinking through several associations such as: "Making mistakes is important if I am to learn the right way. Because I have been so upset about making mistakes, and down on myself for them, I have been less prepared to take the risks necessary to achieve big things."*

*I realised this was another way of getting down on myself, so I tapped on …*

"I accept myself even though I haven't been prepared to take risks due to fear of making a mistake ..."

"I accept myself even though I have not yet achieved enough due to my fear of making mistakes ..."

*All of a sudden I was transported back in my mind to my Year 6 classroom where the motto was "If you're going to do something, do it properly", a guideline which the teacher repeatedly implored everyone to follow.*

*I immediately did a round of tapping on this class motto, "Even though if you're going to do something you should do it properly, I fully and completely accept myself.'*

*This brought back memories of the teacher's exasperation when anyone failed to measure up, it also allowed me to see the parts of the statement that did serve me and how I also took on some meanings that didn't serve me.*

*I then recalled a critical incident in that classroom where I had received 49.5 out of 50 for the weekly test — the highest mark anyone had achieved all year — and yet I copped a lot of criticism from both the teacher and my parents for falling short by making a "silly mistake".*

*I reviewed this incident in my mind and tapped on the parts that held negative emotional intensity. I also applied tapping to the following thoughts:*

"Even though I made a silly mistake ..."

"Even though their criticism hurt ..."

"Even though I must do things properly or else ..."

*After this I was able to go back to my work and be quite productive. As my fear of making mistakes had been relieved, I found myself no longer self-editing or self-critical to the same degree. And over the next few weeks I realised that I was able to achieve more in my work because I was no longer as fearful of making mistakes.'*

## AN EXERCISE FOR SELF-ACCEPTANCE

To take your own journey to self-acceptance further, locate all the childhood experiences where you learned that you were not acceptable and apply EFT/SET to them. Use the 'Tell the Story' or 'Run the Movie' techniques, stopping to tap on any part of the memory that makes you feel intense, until you can review the whole event without experiencing the same emotional intensity.

As you play the memories through, try to identify the beliefs you learned or the generalisations you took from the experience that are now limiting you and tap on those too. Repeat the entire belief statement at each tapping point. Keep tapping on this until the belief statement feels less emotionally intense. Follow the links to other incidents and the thoughts that come up with them, applying tapping to each in turn. Apply the 'Tell the Story' or 'Run the Movie' techniques to them as appropriate.

## ADDRESSING SELF-ACCEPTANCE ISSUES

If you have trouble with the self-accepting part of the EFT set-up statement then this is a cue to treat the issue of self-acceptance for yourself. Rather than just trying to skirt around your unwillingness to make the self-accepting statement and find some way to proceed with treating the 'problem', we believe it is worthwhile to focus on your non-acceptance as a problem in its own right.

Often, when people use EFT/SET and get relief on a particular problem, say a phobia, they also tend to get a burst of energy and self-acceptance. However, lack of self-acceptance seems such a pervasive thing that it usually isn't long before their concerns have centred on a different problem. *You now have a different reason for not accepting yourself!* The fact that we move on to different problems in a constant manner is not the challenge; the challenge is that our lack of self-acceptance underlies them all — it is the one constant. We believe we all need to target this directly. In Steve's case, it has been a very fruitful area of self-discovery and personal growth.

## Sources of Low Self-Acceptance

We do not accept ourselves as we are for many reasons. One reason is because we have conflicting parts inside us jostling for prime position. Winston Churchill called this process 'internal civil war'!

When we query clients on the reasons why they don't accept themselves, these are the things they typically come up with (you might like to consider how many of these apply to you):

I do not accept myself because:

- I have this bad problem.

- I do not do the things I should do.

- I do things I shouldn't do.

- I did something bad in my past.

- I think thoughts that are bad and evil.

- I have not achieved the level of success I should.

- My performance at some test/task is/was below standard.

- I don't know what I want, or the best way to proceed.

*Emotional Roots*

Typically, the non-self-acceptance has roots in past childhood experiences where a significant person (mother, father, teacher, peer, mentor) did not accept you. The generalisation becomes 'Since they did not accept me, I cannot be acceptable'. This is a strong common theme. Invariably there are several key incidents where your negative view of self was 'learned'.

Since your negative self-assessment is frequently grounded in past experiences where a significant adult rejected you, or did not validate your feelings or behaviours, this provides strong justification for ongoing negative self-evaluation. To use a metaphor provided by social psychologist Robert Cialdini, these negative experiences become the legs holding up a negative belief table based around your unworthiness and self-criticism. If we detach the legs then the belief table is no longer supported, and therefore the belief is no longer strongly held.

Thus, treating your past experiences that have gone together to create your key negative belief is one very powerful way of affecting your current self-evaluation. It is also important to treat the almost God-like status which you may have afforded your parents and teachers at the time, because you were looking at them from the perspective of a child. Reducing their status reduces the power of their pronouncement or the assessment implied by their action or inaction.

Past experiences can be identified and treated as mini-traumas, using the 'Run the Movie' and 'Tell the Story' techniques. Treat until you can relate the event without experiencing any emotional intensity. Also treat the generalisations associated with the experiences by stating these at each tapping point (e.g. 'I'm not good enough …'). Make the statement and feel how true it feels, then apply EFT/SET and consider the new rating. Also check how much emotional intensity the statement provokes, and consider the new rating of intensity following treatment. Typically this will be much less.

*Challenges in Current Time*
You may be holding onto a negative self-assessment as a form of self-protection. You may fear that without this, you will be challenged in dealing with life. You may even believe, as Steve did, that if you accept yourself as you are, you will give up on your quest for self-improvement! You could actually see the self-deprecation as useful and self-acceptance as undesirable. One way in which these challenges can be addressed is by tapping alternately on both sides of the continuum (self-acceptance is bad versus self-acceptance is good; I'll stop achieving versus I can happily achieve, etc).

# Tapping Into the Power of Now

Some years before Steve had these experiences and wrote these articles on self-acceptance, he recalled being in a therapy session with Frank Farrelly. He was agonising over an apparent double bind between family and career. He couldn't work out how he could be successful in his career AND be there for his family. Either way he felt guilty, because he wasn't doing enough. It was a real dilemma. Here he continues his story:

*'Right in the middle of my searching for answers, I turned to Frank questioningly about how I might resolve the dilemma. He looked me straight in the eye and said, "Why don't you try a little self-*

*acceptance?" It was as if he had hit me in the face with a wet fish, breaking my problem trance in an instant. "What does that have to do with anything?" was my reaction. Turns out it had everything to do with it …*

*I had been caught up in the complexity of trying to resolve the apparent double bind in my own inner representation of the problem, then along comes Frank crashing through my consciousness with something that seemed to be right out of left field. "Why don't you try a little self-acceptance?" Now I realise his statement, which has never left me, wasn't out of left field at all, it was right over the home plate. Self-acceptance is where it's at.*

*The biggest problem I had was how I felt about myself — and no matter which way I turned with it, that lack of self-acceptance would inevitably follow many of my decisions and actions.'*

There are so many different layers and levels to the self-acceptance dilemma, and we don't have the space to focus on all of them here, so we'll focus for a moment on one of the key components, and that is the unwillingness to be where you are, to start from where you are, being the person you are now right now (i.e. less than perfect), and to act from that point.

As long as you refuse to accept where you are, and who you are, you cannot come to the point of your power. The point of your power is right here right now. It is the point from which all future actions derive, and from which your power to change things flows. A wise person once said you can go anywhere in the world you want to go as long as you are willing to start from where you are.

But you may not want to be where you are if it is a painful place, like when you have experienced a loss. You want to be somewhere else, away from the pain, the place you *should* be.

And you don't want to be who you are when you have been behaving in ways you'd rather not and doing things you 'shouldn't be doing'. You want to be the new and improved version of yourself, 'every movement a picture of grace'.

But the only place you can really start from is where you are, with the resources you have right now. You cannot be where you are and be someone other than the person you are.

Only you, as you are, can start to become what you may be. Starting from who you are and where you are and what you are. Now.

This is another area where the wording in the set-up statement as used in EFT can be valuable:

**'Even though I shouldn't be where I am, I am here ...'**

Eckhart Tolle, author of *The Power of Now*, asks what could be more futile than to create inner resistance to something that already is. When we do this, we are trying to oppose life itself. His prescription, which has brought peace to many people worldwide, is to surrender to what is, and say 'yes' to life. When you do this, life starts working for you rather than against you.

When you experience inner resistance to what is, start tapping. When you think that where you are is not good enough, start tapping. When you think that WHO you are is not good enough, start tapping. Until you come to where you are now, back to yourself, no movement and no change is possible.

So start tapping on the fact that you ARE here, in a place where, perhaps, you don't even want to be. It's not wonderful, but it is where you are. You may feel bad about it, but it is where you are.

The key here is to bring the tapping — and your attention — into the NOW. Focus on what you are doing NOW, on the feelings you are having in your body, and the thoughts you are having NOW. And as you continue to tap, you just may start to come to terms with who and what and where you are. And the moment you accept where you are, then you can start to do something about changing.

Milton H. Erickson is a therapist who is famous for joining, rather than opposing, the world views and beliefs of his clients. In one of his teaching tales, recorded in the book *Phoenix: Therapeutic patterns of Milton H. Erickson* (co-authored by David Gordon and Maribeth Meyers-Anderson), Erickson tells the story of John, a psychiatric patient who continually pestered everybody on the ward with the statement that he didn't belong there. Erickson instructed the staff to reply, 'But you are here!' every time John made this statement. After about six months of this, John finally responded, 'I KNOW I'M HERE!!' and Erickson was able to say to him, 'Now that you are here, what do you want to do about leaving here?' Not long after this, John was able to be discharged from the hospital and make a successful transition back into the community. This is the sort of powerful result that can follow from first accepting where you are and then focusing on where you want to go and how to get there. But it is the acceptance that must come first ...

## Using Energy Techniques in Relationships

A relationship is a devotional friendship, where the wounds from criticism are healed over time by compassion and acceptance.

Interestingly enough, according to Dr John Gottman, the number one predictor of difficulty in marriage is the bad habit of constant criticism. You experience a relationship according to your own beliefs about the way things should be — your 'rules'. And then your partner has the gall to break them! (And vice versa, of course, although this seems like a minor issue to you.

The most important way to use EFT/SET here is to help yourself handle the upset feelings that arise when you are in conflict with someone you care for. While these feelings are not 'wrong' in themselves, they can be very strong, triggering other 'bad' feelings from the past (which can be a lot stronger than those from the initial problem). Often this leads to a loss of *friendship*.

If you treat the negative feelings that get in the way of a solid friendship, then you can work later on resolving those issues. That will help the relationship. In a marriage these include learning to communicate effectively, knowing how to help and please your partner, and building up tolerance and acceptance.

The best reason to work on *yourself* is because you realise that you share the problem if one of you is upset — and you do what you can do about it first. Of course, you are always tapping on your own 'emotional stuff' as you follow this strategy, regardless of whatever work your partner 'should' be doing. You have your own work to do in just *accepting* what is happening without approving of it, or agreeing with it.

The bottom line is that it's all really your personal work on your own reactions, regardless of the problem 'in the relationship'. We suggest you 'graft' EFT/SET (mainly continual tapping) on to your behaviours and reactions as an initial approach. This is self-acceptance in action. Be very persistent about helping yourself; give yourself some time to make a shift. You did not stumble into this problem overnight, and it will take some time to resolve it, too. That's where the continual tapping will be most helpful.

Using EFT/SET persistently is often highly effective in interrupting the blaming and fault-finding downward spiral. With this simple method, you can gain some initial relief, and then start to correct the deep-seated hurt and pain more directly than by thinking about it or talking about it. (It's too hard to think very clearly in those circumstances, anyway.)

Another way to consider using EFT/SET is as a good 'first-aid' response. When partners already have goodwill and a positive intention and history, EFT/SET used automatically in this way can reverse the outcome of a lot of marital accidents.

One objection to using EFT/SET for these common hurts is that they could lead to your feeling relaxed about a legitimate issue of abuse if you are on the receiving end. Now, really, this is possible only if you have severe personal problems to begin with! It would show up as, for example, your feeling like you 'didn't matter' or that you are 'always in the wrong anyway'.

We would still use EFT/SET in this situation, since they are very likely to lead to greatly increased self-esteem over time. When EFT/SET do their magic to your dysfunctional feeling–reactions (everybody has some!), there's little danger that you will become too saintly or forgiving for the wrong reasons; you do not lose your commonsense or your time-tested ability to say or do the wrong thing occasionally!

We are not suggesting that all personal problems can be easily solved, nor that one person can necessarily solve a 'two-person' problem. But this kind of self-help is vital whether you use professional assistance in your relationship or not.

## HOW DO I USE SET WITH A RELATIONSHIP ISSUE?

Far more useful than finding the right words to say (as in EFT), is the idea of using a lot of tapping (as in SET) at the 'hot point' of your frustration. Here are some shortcuts in dealing with the suffering:

- Focus on your body discomfort — where you feel these feelings (if you can identify a place).

- Apply SET at length until you do experience a 'shift' and some relief.

- Apply SET even if you don't know exactly what you are doing — it is your own deep hurt that you are treating. Treat yourself first and see what is left afterwards.

- Focus, for example, on 'my tears', 'this empty feeling', 'stomach emotion', 'my heartache'. Tap on the words that were said, the 'look' that was on your partner's face, or how 'stupid' you feel for being in this position. This kind of focus happens naturally when you allow your feelings to be there without struggling to get rid of them.

- When things have settled down, another very useful strategy is to use opposite statements on alternate points while tapping: 'This is right for me' on the first point; 'This is wrong for me' on the second, and so on. Or you could say: 'I know I'm right' on the first, and 'But it's not working' on the second, and 'I must keep going' on the third. You 'allow' the negative like this.

- Do more tapping for the feelings about injustice, unfairness, resentment and unforgiveness standing in the way of your 'recovery'.

- Keep doing continual tapping and see what happens.

Creatively ignore the hurt if possible. Your partner is going to hurt you sometimes — *just as you will hurt them sometimes*. Apologise if necessary. Negotiate the problem. Reconnect. Life is short.

**Example of EFT/SET for a Relationship Issue**

This is a composite example of how to use EFT/SET in treating a relationship issue. The presenting problem is the frustration of a wife who 'can't trust' her husband, as a result of repeated broken promises.

The couple sits together in a counselling session, both have learned EFT/SET, and it is her turn to talk about her grievance. We ask her to tap on her facial points whenever she feels intense about the situation, as it is important to take up every opportunity to 'treat as you go', and to end such a session with as many sequences of tapping completed as comfortably possible. We also ask the husband, this time, to tap for relief, if he needs to, while she talks — but to be silent while she is talking.

She says: 'He's always saying one thing and doing another ... I get my hopes up, but he never follows through. He lies! I'm sick of it!'

Now we ask permission to go further with this, and request that she look into her husband's eyes while she follows our actions and repeats these words:

'Even though you lie to me ... and let me down ... and dash my hopes ... part of me still loves you.'

'Even though you say one thing and do another, I do my best to handle you.'

'Even though you never follow through ... and I'm really sick of it ... and maybe there is no answer to this ... I'm going to find an answer if I can.'

Now she taps on the seven basic shortcut points while saying: 'You lie. You let me down. I can't stand it. I can't stand you. I have no hope. Maybe we can't make it. I don't know what to do.'

While these statements are intuitive, they also pace the wife's experience, and she knows from our inquiries after the sequences that she can adjust their accuracy if she wants to (instant feedback). We find that all such statements have come up at one time in the mind of a distressed spouse ('speaking the unspeakable' according to Frank Farrelly).

Typically, by using the paradox of worsening the situation, strong emotions surface and release. She would typically cry or get angry.

We now say: 'Keep on tapping on the points' (it's very important to keep tapping with strong feelings, as this is the antidote).

Now we switch to the body: 'If you had to name a place in your body where these feelings might collect, where would it be?' The answer might be over the heart. We say: 'Put one hand over that place and focus all your attention underneath — as if those feelings have a shape and you could connect with that shape, and touch it.' We all keep tapping in silence so as not to interrupt the process with words, and to give some time and space to the obvious hurt.

Sometimes this can take a few minutes. Often we will ask if we can help by doing some of the tapping for her, and if the answer is 'yes', we will use the hand points (and wrist points); Gary Craig has done this tapping for clients consistently in all of his EFT trainings and it is a beautiful gesture and assistance in the right hands.

When things settle down, we check the body sensations and their intensity, and repeat some sequences on 'chest emotion' or 'heart feeling', if necessary. It's not vital to get such intensities down to zero as they represent a big picture which is unfolding, so aspects of the problem pop up in many guises, and you deal with them as they do.

We like to emphasise the bizarre aspects of loving and hating someone simultaneously (the 'good' partner and the 'bad' partner), and making molehills into mountains so that eventually even the client finds it hard to agree that they have teamed up with the 'worst person in the world', or that their 'shocking bad judgement' in saying 'yes' to him means that they are a 'very slow learner'! (Note the natural humour that comes with these 'agreements'.)

A healthy dispute commences, which we can humorously refute, as if we are on the side of her nightmare, as if we agree that it's really too hard or hopeless (or whatever she said when she was steamed up). We tap on either side of the belief system, emphasising the good or the bad, but would exaggerate that polarity to an uncomfortable degree. This is a slippery situation for the client to respond to.

For maximum effect, she can follow a sequence of tapping where the good and the bad are presented alternately with each point! The 'good' news will usually have an echo in the client's belief structure, which is a disbelieving or cynical opposite response, while the 'bad' news is treated anyway in the usual manner. A lot of negativity is processed very quickly with such accelerated confusion. That confusion exists anyway in the love/hate dichotomy but, after EFT/SET, it settles to tolerable levels.

While doing the initial statement, we would have the wife say (looking at her partner): 'Although part of me hates what you do, I don't hate you — but I do sometimes, and I hate feeling like that; and even if all that is true, I accept myself deeply and completely … I accept myself, even though it's very hard to accept myself as a wife when I have these hateful feelings … I love and forgive myself even though it might be a very long time before I'll do that for you, considering your track record.'

Now she taps on the points, moving to the next point with each phrase: 'I love you. I don't love you. I hate you. Part of me loves you. Part of me hates you. I only love the good you. I really hate the bad you.'

We progress in the session by testing the original propositions and complaints for emotional intensity. If things have shifted to positive and life-affirming directions, a guaranteed way to further the work required is to get the husband to proffer some of his favourite excuses or rationalisations. With the wife's response you will find more work to be done!

Later in therapy the husband has a turn, and the couple can do all of the above strategies together, simultaneously or sequentially, straight or paradoxically. Are we having fun yet?

Of course, as the counsellor or therapist, you need excellent rapport and loving kindness in your empathic resonance. We also think you need to be able to tolerate the ambiguity and ambivalence involved in 'making the problem worse' in a creative and loving way. For some, this emphasis would go against the grain of positive thinking (or the pursuit of happiness in some countries). It might even be unconstitutional.

## ON 'BEING RIGHT' IN RELATIONSHIPS

*'Out beyond ideas of wrongdoing and rightdoing there is a field.*
*I'll meet you there.'* Rumi

It is quite gratifying to be in the right. To be superior to those lesser beings who have not understood how things are meant to be, and whose behaviour is far more childish than your own. To never make a mistake — apart from the semi-permanent one of not 'getting' what your partner or family really needs from you! And the universal mistake of not listening to others in the first place. As Frank Farrelly says: 'Don't tell me the truth — leave me with my distorted perceptions.'

But if you are always trying to be 'in the right' in a committed relationship, then you can easily make your partner feel 'one-down' and 'wrong'. Your mind even tells you that you can hurt yourself, or your best friend, and get away with it! The result is a life-denying stalemate where all energy in the relationship is blocked. The resulting feelings of anger, hurt and helplessness for both are best treated initially with EFT/SET as 'first aid' (regardless of the cause or person at fault).

The great intensity of those emotions makes a relationship the 'crucible' of change (this is therapist David Schnarch's metaphor about marriage). It also makes techniques like EFT/SET the most useful kind of self-help possible. With each 'opportunity' there is for getting hurt by the thoughtless behaviour of others, you can tap and avoid the pointless fighting and retribution you might usually indulge in. After treating the body problem in this way (remember, EFT/SET are body–mind techniques), it is far more likely that your mind will be settled and ready to negotiate or learn to change.

## Criticism

Here's a sure way to ruin your relationship: be a critic. Of all the relationship poisons, this is the deadliest. Over time, it is guaranteed never to improve the quality of your life.

EFT/SET are the most useful antidotes to this poison. Using EFT/SET initially doesn't solve the problem; instead, they help you to get straight emotionally first. When you can be more emotionally balanced, both parties can confront the truths of the situation more evenly.

The urge to criticise and blame comes from deeply felt ideas about the world and how it should be. There are two kinds of people in the world: those who can tolerate crumbs in the bed, and those who can't (actually, it's those who think there are two kinds of people in the world and those who don't). As such, the hurt feelings are your own and they are *triggered* by others — not necessarily caused by them. Persistence and more persistence is the key in using tapping to treat the deep anxieties and fears underlying your critical actions. Professional help can accelerate this process if you are not getting anywhere.

## ACCEPTANCE OF BOTH SIDES

If accepting yourself or others takes some mental gymnastics, because you feel that first you must be faultless, or they must change, then go ahead and be inconsistent. Your mind always wants you to choose between good and bad — in a world where everybody is a balance of both qualities, and relationships are a compromise. Self-acceptance is one of the keys to dealing with this complexity. Using your intuition to promote whatever will work (e.g. goodwill and friendship) is another. EFT/SET treat much of the resulting mental discomfort, if you use them persistently.

But whose values will prevail in the relationship? This is a game which you could play all your life in an attempt to preserve what you consider to be the 'truth'. The real truth is that if this game hurts your partner then you are both going to suffer — and that cannot be a good thing. Satisfied men all over the world have realised that women contribute to relationships and families, so such values need to be honoured and to prevail in the home — but that subject is a book in itself.

Work on your own faults first. It is because of grace and kindness in the world that you are forgiven for being 'wrong'. Don't make the mistake of letting your mind run the show when happiness is at stake. Whatever puts a smile on the face of those you care for should be on your agenda. Learning to compromise and to back each other requires a lot of positive feeling and strength. EFT/SET help to minimise the drain on our energies caused by worry. Of course, you can use them for the difficulties in any relationship, such as extended family issues and workplace problems — as long as you realise you are treating first your own reactions to what has happened.

The Buddhist scholar Jack Kornfield has written a book called *After the Ecstasy, the Laundry: How the heart grows wise on the spiritual path*. He tells many amusing stories about what happens after enlightenment to those who have families and relationships — and the difficulties that bring them down to earth in a hurry. What have you gained if it can't be put into practice every day with those you love? Of course, there is much to do in negotiating family life. Some habits and faults are never going to change.

If you can imagine a world where you are treated so well, so kindly and so graciously by someone who thinks the best of you, then naturally you will reciprocate. Nelson Mandela once said: 'If you treat people with impeccable integrity and honesty, then that is how they will treat you.' Do you really have the right to criticise others? Use EFT/SET to help yourself to move beyond your limiting negative beliefs about the world. Start at home.

## WHAT WOULD LOVE DO HERE?

Relationship work is sometimes fraught with peril due to the painful emotional reactions unleashed by nagging, struggling, fighting and enduring the partner's 'doing what they do'. This is far worse than merely a 'wrinkle in the great silk sheet of life'. Misery and divorce are common.

When you feel threatened, you retaliate. Your instincts work against you when you feel threatened by your partner (they may not wish to threaten you, but you feel it anyway). Harville Hendrix, author of *Getting the Love You Want: A guide for couples*, explains such subjective fear and anger. He considers that your primitive 'reptilian brain' is activated by the event. You decide it is *not safe*. Part of you wants to lash out and deal with the danger to your self-esteem by attacking, or running away, or submitting (the three primitive reactions). It doesn't feel 'natural' in this context to treat yourself when you have been hurt by another person. When faced with this situation, ask yourself:

'Did they mean to do it?' (Have I lost my best friend? Is he/she the enemy now?)

'How am I going to react?'

There is usually little time for thought in such a situation, as your emotional reactions tend to develop quickly. Emotional violence, including feelings of rage, self-harm, helplessness and depression, results all too frequently. There are few reliable ways to achieve relief when such primitive feelings rise up. EFT/SET provide 'first aid' par excellence.

The radical part of this program involves asking yourself quickly the third, but important, question:

'What would love do here?'

When you experience the immediate effect of this question you will also feel your negative blocks in full force. It's like telling two men fighting to 'stop and shake hands'! The advice might be good but the feelings may be too strong for everyone involved to 'do the right thing'.

Apply EFT/SET to your negative feelings. Focus on your body discomfort — *where* you feel these feelings (if you can identify a place). Focus on any of the following thoughts and apply SET, or if using EFT you could think or say: 'I accept myself deeply and completely even though ...'

'This is too much.'

'I can't deal with this.'

'This is the last straw.'

'It's happened again.'

'He/she promised me.'

'My world is collapsing.'

'I can't live like this.'

'I said never again.'

'This is unforgivable.'

All these statements could be used as part of direct focus (typically triggering 'hot' feelings) in SET, if they were used as guiding ideas about the relationship problems.

Tap on any feelings of anger, shame, fear and sadness and follow these feelings — and any impressions and associated memories if you can — while they are fresh. With SET it is often the 'doing' that helps rather than the 'thinking about' or 'naming' the problem. Be pleased you are 'dealing with' major upset feelings. This action is the psychological equivalent of applying pressure to a bleeding wound while staying calm.

When you do feel calmer you have the chance of coping the best you can. You are 'breaking the chain' of your couple problem by helping yourself. You then decide about further resolution, action or help, based on your best judgement of what actually happened. You may also have had enough of any mistreatment. There are new possibilities for the two of you, thanks to the effect of tapping.

In the end the path is lifelong personal work on your toxic reactions (no matter what the trigger). EFT/SET are the natural antidotes.

## SPECIALISED COUPLE TECHNIQUES USING SET

While a couple often needs help from someone skilled in relationship problems, there is much that you could do yourselves if the issues are not too big. If they are, we suggest that you get professional help, regardless of knowing about tapping. In that case, tapping will help very much as 'homework'. The following strategies are suitable for ordinary upsets that all couples go through.

### Working Together Using Tapping

This framework is based on the values of friendship, goodwill and commonsense in a relationship. We suppose that if all these qualities were operating properly then, logically, there would be no couple problems! But every couple has 'stuff' so they could benefit from using EFT/SET. Bliss won't happen automatically.

Continual tapping in SET is a central part of the procedure. It helps you work on yourself for a hurt 'triggered' by your partner. It interrupts habitual patterns. It is first aid too. All these tapping techniques bypass the judgemental mind.

The magic of SET in relationship work can be brought out by three simple techniques. These techniques are single, joint and unison ones. *Single* techniques are useful early on as difficult issues are brought up. *Joint* techniques help to 'share' the problem in a way that is natural. *Unison* techniques are for the end of a session *after* work has been done on any irritations and resentments. These irritations fuel the struggle of unhappy couples and must be cleared before the unison techniques can be used.

## Single Techniques

Both partners can each be using continual tapping. It is a relaxing and self-soothing practice. Take it in turns to say what's important to you.

If you are listening, tap because you are involved in the drama and the history. If you are talking, it is important to you, so keep tapping.

If there is blame and fault in the session, the recipient will definitely need tapping to stay 'centred'.

## Joint Techniques

All relationship problems are shared so all tapping should be a joint activity too. This is best for 'heavier' issues.

When, for example, a spouse wants to say something important, or to apologise or make amends, s/he 'lends' her/his arm, and the other *taps continually on her/his finger/hand points as s/he talks*. Couples can do this face to face or sitting side by side. The listening partner acts as a 'mirror' to the words but stays calm with the help of SET. This is true 'active listening'. S/he must *say nothing* and not interrupt the partner at this point. S/he stops when s/he has said enough.

The only job for the listening partner is to do the tapping on her/his own points while listening. This helps the first partner to feel 'heard'. It is hard for the listening partner to say nothing, but instead of disputing the issue — with a predictable reaction and counterreaction — s/he bears with it and listens. This is a different experience. Note that s/he is getting some energy point stimulation by the very act of doing the tapping. Of course, they may take it in turn.

*Unison Techniques*

Unison techniques are best used when there is sufficient relaxation after tapping on any problems. There is no rush.

Here, the partners look silently into each other's eyes while both receive tapping from the other only on the face points.

*While doing this, each partner sends the greatest love or wish for the other.* This is a potent suggestion. They should remember the time when they first got together and realised how special they could be. Nothing was too much trouble. They should recall any promises made to each other.

It is a beautiful thing to find love still fresh, despite everything.

# Using Energy Techniques for Peak Performance

Peak performance is no accident. It is usually the result of a powerful vision and a workable plan put into action over time. However, there are some definite strategies and mental/emotional patterns that can accelerate your success. EFT/SET can be applied very effectively in business, sports and, indeed, any area of endeavour to enhance performance and improve results.

We have applied EFT/SET very effectively to enhance performance in a range of sports and business applications. You can use these energy tools in a variety of ways to enhance your performance. These include:

- Overcoming any internal blocks you have to performing at your peak and achieving your ultimate goals (see page 190).

- Expanding your comfort zone. EFT/SET can assist you to progressively become more comfortable with success at a level beyond your current performance. This requires identifying the current comfort level and then tapping on the idea or the intention to 'be' at a different level of performance. This can be combined with the instructions for 'Connecting with Success' (see page 187).

- Overcoming specific performance blocks, for example, the situations that 'bug' you or affect you negatively in your area of performance. These might be specific situations, such as chipping onto the green for golfers, having to face up to a particular opposition player in any sport, or having to hit a game-winning shot in basketball. In business, this might be having to present a speech, or presenting your proposal to the board, or cold-calling customers.

- To clear the negative effects of a less-than-perfect performance or a setback. This can include specific problems within a performance situation, such as having just hit a poor shot, receiving the news that you just lost a particular business account, or experiencing a rejection from a potential client or customer in a sales situation.

- To assist you to get 'into the zone', a state of maximum focus and concentration prior to and during performance. Tapping can be used in combination with self-talk and visualisation focused on the outcome you desire. For example, a baseball hitter might have an intention to 'see the ball, hit the ball'. Just prior to going up to bat, s/he might repeat such words to her/himself while tapping. This would have been practised many, many times prior to the match mentally, and combined with regular physical practice situations.

- In practice, EFT/SET can be used to improve your adoption of a particular skill. For example, tapping can be combined with mental practice and visualisation to see yourself performing a move perfectly, then connecting with the feeling of that and ultimately gaining the kinesthetic (felt) sense of completing the move perfectly — along with the inner confidence that it is possible for you. Use the 'Connect with Success' technique (see page 187), and apply those instructions to any skill you want to develop or improve.

- Overcoming injury. EFT/SET can be effectively used to assist recovery from injury, and also to deal with the emotions that having such setbacks can cause a professional athlete.

- Addressing self-image/identity issues and treating any negative self-beliefs, which could hinder peak performance, as well as assisting you to develop a success identity.

- Addressing core values, ironing out conflicts in values, and uncovering your 'true' values, which are your most important states of being.

- Ensuring that your goals are aligned with your core 'true' values and charting a path which, to you, represents ultimate success.

Below are two testimonials from athletes who have used the Energy Techniques to achieve peak performance. These accounts will inspire you with the potential these methods hold.

*Australian Baseball League Pitcher of the Year Pat Ahearne*
[Note: In baseball statistics, the Earned Run Average is one of the main yardsticks by which pitchers are measured. It is the mean of earned runs given up by a pitcher per nine innings pitched. Generally, an ERA around 3.0 is considered better than average. An ERA below 2.0 is very rare.]

*'As anyone who has competed in athletics can say, the difference between the average athlete and the elite player is much more mental than physical. In an effort to bring my mental preparation for baseball to the same level as my physical preparation, I was introduced to EFT by Steve Wells, a psychologist based in Perth, Australia. Before working with Steve, I was able to perform well in training and some of the time in games, but I wanted to access my best performances more often and in the most pressure-filled situations.*

*Steve and I worked together using EFT to lessen or eliminate the mental and emotional barriers preventing my consistently producing my best games as a pitcher. The results were astounding. I had more consistency, better command of my pitches, and accomplished it in big games with less mental effort.*

*[In 46 innings pitched prior to using EFT, Pat achieved an ERA of 3.3, which is quite a reasonable performance. However, in 41.1 innings pitched after using EFT his ERA plummeted to 0.81, an incredibly low figure.]*

*Using EFT, I found the mental edge that raises an athlete from average to elite. I used the techniques to capture the MVP (Most Valuable Player) of the Perth Heat and the Australian Baseball League Pitcher of the Year awards.*

*I am so amazed with the effectiveness of EFT that I've made it an important part of my baseball routine.'*

## Sydney TAB Swift and Australian Netball Representative Catherine Cox

'EFT got me through the toughest part of my sporting career. Being an athlete and spending your whole life trying to be the best you can be in a sport you love is gratifying. As you may or may not know netball is not a professional sport, so to be able to commit so much time and dedication into something, you really have to love what you're doing! And I do ... now!!

Netball had always been something I loved. I loved the feeling of being out there on the court enjoying my skills and the skills of the team around me! It was always something I was extremely confident about until I made the move to a new team that needed a bookend, a focal point! A team that was relying on me to pull them through the dark times and create some wins. Being on court in front of this new crowd and new team I felt an unbelievable amount of pressure! I HAD to be a superstar or these new people would wonder why I'm here! I HAD to get some wins on the board for my new team to show I WAS having an impact here!

It was the start of the second year that this pressure and lack of confidence came to a real problem point and as a shooter it was obvious. I had always been a player that went out there and just played and, all of a sudden, I was made to think about every move I made and every thought I was having. I started to over-examine myself constantly and lost confidence even more drastically. Thoughts like "I have to get this shot in or people will think I'm not good enough" or "I don't want the ball because I don't want to have to shoot it. I could miss." My shooting percentages dropped significantly but what's worse is that I no longer wanted to be on the court playing the game I loved. All my confidence was lost!

The final turning point after weeks of telling myself the feeling *would go away came in an International Test match against New Zealand. I had been given the opportunity to start the game, which showed a lot of belief in me by my coaching staff. The feeling I had, however, was sickness. I couldn't think of anything worse than being out in front of a crowd watching the two best netball teams in the world going head to head. What if they think I'm not good enough and that I shouldn't be there? I returned home prepared to do whatever it took to sort myself out or I was going to have to give up the sport I used to love so much.*

*I had never, ever been a fan of sports psychologists and when someone mentioned this new technique called Emotional Freedom Techniques that a man named Steve Wells specialised in, I was more than sceptical, to say the least! During my first meeting with Steve I was truly at the bottom of the barrel in terms of confidence and couldn't believe that my fear of never playing and enjoying the game again would ever go away! It was weighing me down so much it couldn't possibly just go away!*

*To be honest my first experience with EFT was horrible because it was all about confronting my fears head on and saying them out loud! Something I had yet to do! It was bad enough thinking about them! I remember crying so much and struggling to breathe thinking to myself this man [Steve] is in way over his head! Surely he's not had to deal with something this bad before?*

*[Steve: When Catherine arrived for that first session she was in a very upset state and her issues were really close to the surface. Since she knew about EFT and was highly motivated we started using the technique almost immediately on the things she was thinking and feeling. While it isn't necessary to always 'confront fears head on', I've found that when someone is 'in' an intense state, the best*

remedy is lots and lots of tapping right then and there. We did a large number of rounds that session, including some tapping while talking and processing the information.]

I got through the first session but the test would not come until I was in the situation I had struggled with all year — on the court. After the session I was still extremely sceptical because I really didn't feel any differently. It was when I hit the court again that I noticed a difference in the way I felt when out there. I was almost looking forward to playing the game, which was a feeling that had been evading me lately. It wasn't a miracle cure by any means, but with so many issues to cover my change wasn't going to happen over night.

I found myself at home practising the technique (certainly not something I would do if I didn't think that maybe this was working). Around that time came my dropping from the Australian team and the time I knew I had to really take hold of this and fix the problem — next year was a Commonwealth Games year and I was going to be there.

[Steve: Catherine's shooting percentage improved from 55 per cent the game before we had our first EFT session (a performance that totally disheartened her and explains her really low state when she arrived at my office) to a brilliant 80 per cent in the game she played after doing EFT. Her percentages remained in the high seventies or better for the remainder of the season and the local newspaper described her as returning to 'the top of her form'. Despite this, the feedback I received through her coach was that Catherine 'thought it might have helped but wasn't convinced'. She didn't return to see me at that time. This is a frustrating thing for a practitioner, *especially since I had seen considerable shifts in her emotional levels in the session AND her performance on court had undergone such a dramatic shift. However, I have learnt from past experience to wait and see in these situations and that's what I did.*

*Early the next year, Catherine contacted me again. She reported that the feeling was still there but was definitely lower in intensity and occurring less frequently than before. She wanted to overcome it completely and reach her goal of being in the Commonwealth Games team.*

*We worked for several sessions on her feeling of being 'in the spotlight' and 'having to perform', and the feeling progressively improved. My basic approach was to get her to focus on the actual game situations that provoked the feeling and apply EFT to those. At one point we also uncovered a childhood experience where she had to perform in a school play and treated that successfully using the 'Run the Movie' technique. We also focused on her ultimate goals of being an established Australian team player and world champion, a goal which, in itself, brought up a lot of pressure to perform. I reframed pressure situations as opportunities both to tease out all aspects of the problem and also because the ability to handle more and more pressure is central to the achievement of such a high goal. We were fortunate that many situations arose during the season in which the games placed a great deal of pressure on her to perform. She handled them admirably using EFT.]*

A few more sessions with Steve and my arranged return to the Sydney TAB Swifts was set for the next season, and things were looking brighter. I made the Commonwealth Games team and was having an extremely happy and productive season with my team. Shooting percentages were back to where they should be and I looked forward to the games each week and being on the court again!

In August at the Commonwealth Games I made the gold medal match, a classic Australia versus New Zealand game and although I didn't get to start, I was given the call to go on at half time. After having to endure watching the first half I was feeling pretty sick as it was shaping up to be a typical 'one goal makes the difference game'.

Knowing that I had to go on and make some sort of an impact I took myself out the back and did a little EFT behind the stands while waiting for the half-time whistle. Lucky I did because it ended up going to double extra over time and although I didn't shoot great statistics that game, I certainly made some goals that really counted, helping Australia to a two-goal win and a gold medal. More importantly, at no stage when I missed a shot did I let it bother me! "So what … I missed a shot, I'll just get the next one in!!" An absolute revelation and all thanks to EFT!

[Steve: The gold medal game was an absolute thriller and Catherine hit some clutch shots from long range in the final few seconds to help Australia make it over the line. She is a true world champion, who was able to achieve her dream with the assistance of EFT.]'

# Connecting with Success

One of the most powerful applications of Energy Techniques is to use them to help you create new possibilities in your life, and to help you achieve your ultimate life goals.

The goals you set will depend on a number of factors, not least of which is the point you are at right now. To use the analogy of an explorer out in the wild: if you are sinking in the swamp, your goal may simply be to get to dry land. Once there, however, and after having rested, you will probably want to see if you can get out of the forest. And once out of the forest, you may want to return to civilisation, or you may see a few mountains you want to climb. And after that, the sky's the limit! Whatever your current situation, EFT/SET can be used to help you to:

- See beyond your existing level.

- Move beyond the limitations and barriers you currently perceive.

- Take the actions necessary to reach your ultimate goals, while you enjoy the journey.

Ultimately, EFT/SET can make the journey to achieving your goals a much smoother one. There are two main ways to use EFT/SET for goal achievement. The first is to use the tools to help you clear away the mental and emotional barriers to your decisions and motivations, in order for you to set and take action towards your goals. The second is to use them to help you to connect more easily with success. These processes are intimately connected, however, so it can help to separate them in practice, as you'll see.

## CLEARING OUT THE NEGATIVES

The minute you set a goal to change things, your unconscious blocks will rise up — often the bigger the goal, the bigger the blocks. Business philosopher Jim Rohn says that the real purpose for the goals we have is to become the kind of person we need to become to overcome the blocks and barriers that inevitably arise.

These barriers are usually beliefs that have been lurking beneath the surface. They will tell you why you 'can't' do that and why you 'aren't good enough' or why 'success is hard work' or why 'you will lose your family if you are successful'. (This last belief is one Steve had and he will discuss a little later how he was able to free himself from it.)

The important thing here is to realise that, when setting goals, it is natural that objections and conflicting feelings come up in your mind–body. For most of our significant goals, there are going to be parts of us pulling in different directions.

Fortunately, you can use EFT/SET to defuse the power of these negative objections. To do this:

1. Identify the barriers — these are things like the reasons why you 'can't' do whatever it is you want to do. Get all the objections out. It may help to write these down as a starting point.

2. Apply EFT/SET to each objection as follows: first state the fear or objection in its strongest form (e.g. 'If I go this way I might fail and embarrass myself', 'We might lose all of our money', etc.).

3. Tap while holding the negative thought or image in mind, or simply focusing on the feeling this causes. Do this for several minutes of continual SET tapping, or several rounds of EFT, then check your feeling. If another aspect has arisen, make that the target of your continual tapping.

4. Visualise both the success scenario (achieving your goal) AND the failure scenario (the worst that could happen) and apply EFT/SET to BOTH of these scenarios. Strangely enough, fear

of success can be just as debilitating as fear of failure. You should treat yourself for both, and more detail on how to do this is provided below.

For some goals, your work on negative objections may need to go further, and a more detailed treatment of what to do in this case is provided later in the book. For many goals, however, this simple process will be sufficient to clear some of the negative energy.

## ACHIEVING YOUR GOALS

One of the keys to goal achievement is to be able to see and feel yourself from the position of having achieved your goals. Tapping can help you to do this by releasing the barriers to being able to access this feeling. Spending some time each day imagining having already achieved your goal, while tapping continually on the energy points, can be very productive indeed. Of course, you can also conduct more specifically targeted EFT rounds or SET continual tapping focused on the specific objections that come up for you when you attempt to connect with the success feeling; however, as you do this process on a daily basis you will find that your success visualisations become more and more real to you, until the achievement of the goal is not only possible, it is inevitable.

'Connecting with Success' is a simple process where you form the intention to connect with the feeling you will have when you have achieved your goal — when you are successful — and use tapping to assist you to create a stronger, more meaningful connection. As you do this, your energy and motivation to achieve your goal, and your 'vibration' as it is often called, will increase. Connecting to your goals in this way draws you towards them energetically and, it could be argued, attracts them towards you also!

This process can also be used to help you to connect with wellness when dealing with physical issues and illness, to bring the feeling and energy of being well into your mind–body.

### The Basic Process of Connecting with Success

The basic process of 'Connecting with Success' involves a few simple steps:

- Define what success is to you; imagine what it will be like when you have achieved your goal.

- Think of that success in the future that you are seeking, then 'step into it' (if you visualise you can literally step into the image in your mind), and allow yourself to feel how it will feel — and keep tapping while holding the intention to connect with the 'success' feelings.

- As you continue and persist with this process, you should start to find it easier and easier to connect with the 'success' feelings, as the negative associations and feelings are naturally desensitised by EFT/SET.

You will almost certainly find that negative objections arise in your mind or tension arises in your body while doing this for the first time. These objections and tensions will likely aim to distract you from your intention to connect with success.

Although it can work to focus in on those objections and tensions and apply tapping to them, we highly recommend separating that kind of 'remedial work' (as in chapters 3 and 4) to a separate tapping session. So in most cases, it is best if you continue tapping on the energy points while maintaining the intention to connect with the real feelings of success *despite your negative objections!* Typically, the continued tapping will ultimately settle down the intense thoughts and feelings.

One helpful tip we often give is to write down your objections as they arise, then put them aside and continue intending to connect with the feeling of success. Any objections will ultimately need to be dealt with and those tensions may still need treatment; however, it is best to address them in a separate tapping session.

Here are some important distinctions to help you in connecting with success:

*Realise that it isn't essential to be able to actually get an image.* The most important part of the process, according to Napoleon Hill (who wrote the classic *Think and Grow Rich*), is to *feel the feeling* of success — to feel what it will feel like when you have achieved your goal. For those who do visualise easily, this means putting yourself 'into the picture', looking out at the world from your own eyes, feeling how it feels to be there. For those who don't visualise easily, while you can learn to do this, the main thing for now is to 'get a sense' of how that will feel being there having already achieved your goal. A quote by motivational speaker and author Mark Victor Hansen might help to explain what we are after here: 'Don't think *of* your goals, think *from* your goals.' I would add the word 'feel' to his quote — think AND feel *from* your goals.

1. Realise that it is common when trying to connect with success for internal resistances to arise. This is good, since when you are 'tuned into' the negative feelings, the tapping is helping to settle these down. However, the danger here is that you will be distracted into focusing too much energy and attention on those thoughts when you are aiming to connect with success. So …

2. Ensure you write down the objections that come up for focused remedial work later. When you are connecting with success and objections arise, write those objections down, then leave them be and continue with your intention until you truly do 'connect with success'.

3. In your remedial tapping sessions, first tap on the negative objections and doubts and fears, then identify specific past events where you learned these limiting associations and tap on them. Think about where you learned that this type of success is not possible for you, or when you started to believe that you are not a successful person, or where you learned about the limits to possibility, generally. Go back and treat those past events by running them through your mind and stopping at any intense points, then begin tapping to bring the emotional intensity down before you continue. Then continue tapping through the entire memory. When you have completed some remedial tapping on negative beliefs and the past events move to point 4.

4. Return to the process of success visualisation and 'Connecting with Success', and notice how much easier it is to connect with the 'success' feelings now that you have removed some of the barriers.

In the moment that you connect with the feeling of having already achieved your goal, you should realise that success is possible, and in that instant it actually starts to manifest in your life. The more you do this and the more often you do this the stronger the attractive process becomes. The tapping helps to settle down the barriers and blocks to believing in the positive possibility. And often, just tapping while holding the intention in mind to connect with success is all that is required to get into this state. Yes, action is still required for success, but when you move forward in a positive success-filled state, action is so much easier and your state also tends to attract to you others who can help you to get there faster.

## Connecting with Wellness

If you have physical issues, such as an illness or injury, you can use the 'Connecting with Success' process to assist your recovery. We call this 'Connecting with Wellness' and it is about connecting with being in a state of health and wellbeing!

The 'Connecting with Wellness' tapping process should be considered as complementary to whatever other treatment your physician has recommended, and it is important when dealing with physical issues to ensure your treatment is conducted in conjunction with an appropriate medical diagnosis and advice from your respected physician. That being the case, you can use the 'Connecting with Wellness' process outlined here to assist your transition back to health and wellbeing. At the very least, even with chronic conditions, we have found that this process can frequently ease many symptoms and, in particular, tends to significantly relieve pain and suffering. For a more complete treatment, combine the 'Connecting with Wellness' approach with the techniques for treating physical issues outlined on page 104.

'Connecting with Wellness' basically involves:

1. Mentally putting yourself into the future doing something you know you will be doing.

2. Seeing yourself *being healthy while doing it.*

3. Holding an intention to connect with the feeling of being well in that situation and place.

You do all this while tapping continually on the energy points.

Note that when you are not well, you may have some difficulty in connecting with the healthy, well feeling. You may have to persist in order to get even just a small part of the feeling. However, it is our experience that getting some of the feeling is absolutely crucial to the success of this pattern — and tapping helps with the parts of you that are objecting and that want to keep pointing out your sick feelings and distracting you into potential alternative negative realities. Once they have been 'settled down' all other positive possibilities and potentials — including your ultimate wellness — can become more real to you.

As an example of using this process, upon returning from one of our workshops in Sydney, Steve had contracted a quite powerful gastrointestinal bug. He had this particularly nasty bug once previously and the results at that time were quite devastating — he was severely incapacitated for over a week with severe diarrhoea and lost 6 kilograms as a result!

This time he did two things that were different. First, he addressed EFT/SET to the stomach feelings and formed the intention for them to heal and assist him to get better. Second, he imagined himself going about the corporate training programs he was booked to conduct over the next two days and put himself into the picture doing well and feeling well in those workshops. Just a couple of brief glimpses of the perspective of being there in the group, being well and doing well, accompanied by only just slightly feeling how that would feel was all that was needed to have a positive effect, and he was able to conduct the workshops with only minimal discomfort. Over the next few days he continued to have low-level symptoms, which eventually abated. Since this time he has used the same process very successfully with himself and also with clients to complement their healing regime. As a result they have reported that it has often accelerated their healing from various conditions.

# Treating Identity Issues

One of the biggest barriers that can hold you back from achieving your goals is a negative self-image or identity. Your identity is basically how you see yourself, and it is made up of a set of beliefs about the kind of person you are. These beliefs help you to be who you are, but they can also act to prevent you from changing this. The challenge is that achieving your ultimate goals may require you to rise above your current perception of your identity.

As Zig Ziglar has stated: 'You will never perform consistently in a manner that is inconsistent with how you define yourself.'

Social psychologist Robert Cialdini says: 'The strongest force in the human personality is our need to remain consistent with how we define ourselves.'

If you can change the way you see yourself, and the way you define yourself, you can change your life.

Here's a simple example of how to do this using EFT/SET. In a corporate group we once worked with was a lady who we'll call Jan. Jan said she did not really have any goals, was quite happy with her life, and was content being the way she was. We are always on the lookout to find a person who, when they say this, we can truly believe because that person will have achieved true victory over self. Until we see and hear total congruence in the person making these statements, we tend to see the words as a cover for fear and a limiting way of thinking about one's self. However, when Jan described herself as an ordinary person her jaw was set and her face was dark.

We looked at the first statement she came up with: 'I'm just an ordinary person' as a current belief. Without objecting to this or passing judgement, we then had her consider the opposite belief: 'I'm an extraordinary person.' We had her say this alternative belief out loud, which to her felt totally untrue, not even desirable. Then we had her do three rounds of EFT. During the first round she focused on her current belief: 'Even though I'm just an ordinary person.' In the second round she focused on the alternative belief: 'Even though I am an extraordinary person'. Finally, in the third round, she focused on each belief interchangeably: 'I'm an ordinary person/I'm an extraordinary person.'

After these three rounds she brightened considerably. She stated excitedly, 'I guess I really AM an extraordinary person.' In addition, her previous way of thinking about herself and her life was dull and unattractive to her now. Lifeless. It didn't feel true at all. And her goals had changed. She was now able to look in directions that she was previously unable to consider — and felt optimistic towards changing her life.

If you want to really change your life, consider how you define yourself. Think of how you would like to be. Apply EFT/SET to the internal objections which arise to the idea of being that NOW. Continue until you get a real feeling of congruency. What usually follows is a real feeling of excitement and an unleashing of personal power and positive potential.

Use EFT/SET to help you create a better life. Use them in a creative way, not just for remedial 'problem removal'. Then you will start to sense your true power and gain access to more of your true potential.

## Overcoming Fear of Success to Achieve Your Goals

Many people think they are suffering a fear of failure when what they really have is a fear of success. In fact, we believe most people are suffering from a fear of success masquerading as a fear of failure. On what basis do we say this? If we ask our clients or workshop participants to think about being successful and having achieved their goal, and then ask them to step into the picture and feel how it will feel, they do not typically report feeling good; most say they feel uncomfortable! They are often hit by massive feelings of anxiety and feeling overwhelmed, and tend to report all sorts of negative thoughts coming up such as, 'I don't deserve this'; 'I'm not good enough'; and so on. This is because they have all sorts of negative associations to being successful. And this is what you want to treat using EFT/SET. Ultimately, unless success — however you define it — makes you feel good, and unless you are attracted towards it, then why would you want to manifest it in your life?

Many people, when we question them about their goals, do not actually have a really positive goal at all when it comes down to it. What they often have is a positive mixed with a negative. The negative is what they believe will come along with the success or that would be required in order for success to happen for them — and, in their mind, both the positive and the negative are linked together so you can't have one without the other.

For example, Steve recently spoke with a gentleman who said that if he were to become successful he would lose his marriage! Well, if that were truly the case, why would he choose to become successful? Steve counselled him to look at creating a new version of success where he stayed in his marriage (since he really wanted to), as his current version of success was really a type of failure. Like many people, he had trouble seeing a new possibility because in his mind the choice was represented as an 'either/or' conflict, where one side had to win and the other had to lose; rather than a 'yes, and …' where both sides can win.

Ultimately, if you have not achieved your goals, then at some level you probably have similarly confused emotional and energetic connections to the idea of success. Seeking to create alignment so that all parts are pulling in the same direction has been a major part of our work with EFT/SET in the area of peak performance. We'd like to outline here some ways of going about treating these blocks and barriers so that you can ultimately go for your goals without feeling blocked or always feeling like part of you is holding back.

One way to begin when treating blocks like this with EFT/SET is to think about what would be the inevitable consequences of being successful for you — both positive *and* negative — and then to treat yourself using EFT/SET for both sides of this conflict.

It's not trendy to acknowledge the negatives that might eventuate from success. We're supposed to assume that all change will be positive. But unless you can prepare yourself for a more realistic picture of success, you will push it away. Unless you can be comfortable with success, you will sabotage it or be unable to handle it. Witness the many people who win the lottery or inherit money only to squander their newfound wealth, and the many athletes who go to the Olympics and get overwhelmed by the hype and aren't able to perform.

Actually, unless your body–mind can handle success and everything it would bring, you will fear it and have part of you acting against allowing it to manifest in your life.

For Steve, increased levels of success mean more opportunities to travel and the inevitable conflict with the needs of his family and his desire to be with them and provide for them. This conflict needed to be resolved otherwise he would always feel divided and guilty whenever he was pursuing one and not the other. He could see himself being very successful on the world stage but miserable without his family.

How to treat such binds? Begin by asking yourself: 'What do I want? What would success look like to me?'

Now consider what positive *and* negative things you associate to being successful. For example:

- If I became financially successful I might not be spiritual.

- If I became successful I might lose my family.

- If I became successful I might have a lot more pressure on me to perform, as well as a lot more pressure on my time and I might not have time to do what I want to do.

Set about treating yourself for your own negative associations and blocking thoughts related to your own version of success. One way to treat these is by simply conducting rounds of EFT/SET while focusing on the belief as you tap on each point. For example, 'If I become financially successful I will not be spiritual.'

The next step is to ask yourself where you learned these beliefs. You can then do EFT/SET on those specific events using the 'Tell the Story' or 'Run the Movie' technique. Do this for all the major experiences you can identify where you had an emotional experience that 'taught' you those beliefs. Typically, after doing this, the negative beliefs will loosen their hold.

A very powerful way to treat beliefs where there is conflict between two apparently opposite sides — such as being successful versus being there for the family, or being spiritual versus being financially successful — is to do alternate tapping on each side of the conflict. The main key to this technique is to come up with the two opposite beliefs and then do alternate rounds of tapping on each one. For example, if you held the belief that financial success might lead to your becoming less spiritual, you might do a round or two of tapping on *'If I become financially successful I will be less spiritual'*. While tapping on this belief statement, focus on all the 'reasons' you can think of from your background and experience — and the events that taught you this — to prove how this could be true. Then do some rounds of tapping on the opposite belief, *'If I become financially successful I will be more spiritual'*, again thinking of reasons why this might be true while tapping on each point.

After you have completed separate rounds of tapping on each belief, you can then do some rounds of EFT/SET where you tap on the opposite statements on each alternate tapping point. For example:

- Eyebrow point: 'Financial success would make me less spiritual.'

- Side of the eye: 'If I were financially successful I could contribute more to worthy causes.'

- Under the eye: 'If I were financially successful I might become greedy.'

- Under the nose: 'Actually I'd be less greedy because I wouldn't be worried about money.'

And so on ...

The idea is ultimately not for either side to 'win' over the other, it is to bring both sides (the conflicting ideas, or opposite points of view) into the light of your awareness, allowing each to provide its message. As you do the tapping on the emotionally attached material on both sides of the continuum, the emotion attached to those ideas is able to move through you, and you reprocess the information through your body–mind. As this happens you tend to gain new perspectives regarding the meaning of those ideas and the past events where you learned them. Ultimately, you tend to rise up to a new level of understanding where you are empowered to see or create a new, more empowering definition of success.

Most people who do this simple process of tapping on opposites find, after the initial period of disorientation or confusion, that they are able to come up with a new alternative, which is far more empowering than either side of the conflict would provide on its own. Instead of having to resolve the double bind, they are able to break out of it by rising above it.

Steve's experience when he went through this process was to realise that he *does* need to be there for his family *and* that he does need to make a difference in the world to be true to his purpose (although ultimately his family does comes first). He also realised that being successful with his family supports him in making a bigger difference in the world, and being successful in the world outside his family enhances the person he brings to his family. Thus, while he still travels, he has set some clear boundaries around how much travel he does; he seeks to leverage the opportunities he has when he does travel; he is starting to identify ways he can make a difference without having to leave home so often; and sometimes he arranges to take his family with him!

Once you have done some tapping on your conflicts and blocking beliefs associated with being successful, it's time to focus on manifestation. Manifestation is where you direct your intention to bring your dreams and goals into reality.

# Manifesting the Life of Your Dreams

In essence, the process of achieving new goals and changing your identity is a process of manifestation, and with EFT/SET you can ultimately manifest the life of your dreams.

The reality is that everyone manifests all the time. We are constantly creating our own reality, bringing ideas into form. The trouble is that most of us are doing this on autopilot, and often manifest negatively. We want to focus here on the process of conscious creation, where we decide to bring into form some new, more positive ways of being and create richer, more meaningful, positive outcomes in our lives. These are some of the most exciting applications of Energy Techniques in our opinion, requiring us to break through our old, limiting beliefs of possibility and allowing us to expand and realise more of our true potential.

As mentioned previously, although the act of consciously deciding to create a new future is one of the most empowering actions you can take, it can also be one of the most challenging because you are instantly confronted by your limitations. These limitations are your beliefs about who you are (your identity beliefs), and your beliefs about possibility, in particular your beliefs about what is possible for you. You may also have specific beliefs that hold you back in any area of life. Many people have negative beliefs about money that hold them back from being able to easily manifest more wealth — this includes beliefs that acquiring money is not spiritual, that making money is hard work, and that rich people are greedy, among others. When you hold these beliefs it can hold you back from being able to move forward in creating wealth and success. The good news is that these beliefs can be treated using the Energy Techniques we have outlined in this book.

When you set goals, your limiting thoughts about possibility are stirred into action. Ultimately, if you don't treat yourself for these limitations, you risk remaining a prisoner of your own version of 'what is', or your current reality. We're particularly interested in those wild ideas about 'what could be' that leap into your mind and crash up against your beliefs about what is possible for you. These are the big, hairy audacious goals that both excite and scare you at the same time. If you have one of those goals in your heart, then please follow through with the following exercises. They are designed to help you to start to move beyond your current limiting beliefs.

## GOALS AND BELIEFS EXERCISE

What is your biggest dream, wish or goal? Whatever it is, accept that it is there for a reason and decide you are going to use this process to help you make it real.

Once you have identified a goal, the crucial next step in the manifestation process is to begin to bring a representation of it into the world. There are many ways of doing this, all of which work differently for different individuals. (The first thing to treat yourself for is the belief that you need to set goals according to someone else's formula — even ours!) Some examples are:

- writing it down

- drawing or painting a picture of it

- saying your goal out loud either to someone or making an audio recording of your goals

- making a three-dimensional representation of your goal like a sculpture, and so on or

- taking some physical action towards your goal, such as sitting behind the wheel of that car you long for.

Putting your ultimate goal out into the world — even just to acknowledge that you wish for it — can, in itself, be a scary proposition, especially if the goal is big enough and crazy enough. We ask ourselves (à la Marianne Williamson and Nelson Mandela), 'Who am I to think I can be/do/have this?'

This thought, and the attendant feelings and associations that come with it, are what we first need to tap on. Apply EFT/SET to any and all thoughts that achieving this is not possible for you; that you are not good enough to have it; and that, for whatever reason, you cannot or will not be able to bring it into being. Example statements here might include:

'I'm not good enough to …'

'I don't have what it takes to …'

'I'm (state your own limitation here — e.g. too old, too young, not smart enough, etc.) to …'

It is important to note that these are all beliefs, and the good news is that they can be treated using the techniques described previously in this book. That is, start by tapping while focusing on the belief itself and any feelings it provokes. Then, if necessary, go to the specific events and past situations where you learned this belief and apply EFT/SET to any negative intensity and associated thoughts and feelings provoked by that event. Do this on all the major events associated with the belief, and then you will usually find that the belief isn't held as strongly and/or doesn't affect you as intensely.

When the belief loses its emotional power, it will no longer be able to hold you back, and you will find it much easier to move towards your goal, even in your mind, as we do in the next step.

Next use the 'Connecting with Success' process as outlined on page 187, where you think about your goal from the perspective of being in it, having already achieved it.

The challenge is to capture the real feeling of how this will be — that's where the power lies. And this is where the tapping can help. So, tap continually on the energy points while you maintain the intention to connect with the success image and feeling. Even seconds per day spent in accessing the feelings of a new reality can pay off in incredible ways.

So take a few moments now to think yourself into this new future where you have already achieved your goal, tapping all the time, until your image of success becomes more real and the feelings of success come into your mind–body.

**Do It Every Day**

We recommend you do this process every day for as long as you can (say for up to half an hour each day). First do a session of 5–10 minutes clearing out the negative objections, followed by a session of 5–10 minutes or more of 'Connecting with Success'.

The more you do this simple two-step process, the more your images of future possibility will start to feel more real, and the more confident you will become that not only can your goal be achieved, but that you can — and will — achieve it.

When you use this process on all of your goals, not only will they begin to feel more achievable, but they will also start to become the reality by which you run your life. Some people may find that a four-step process works best — something like this:

**Step 1:**

Focus on that big, audacious goal of yours. Bring it into your mind.

**Step 2:**

Now do some tapping while focusing on any doubts and objections that come up when you focus on your goal.

**Step 3:**

Now do some tapping on the opposite idea — that you can and will make this goal real. For example: 'I can (state your goal) and I will (state your goal).'

**Step 4:**

Now mentally go to the position of having achieved your goal and tap while intending to 'connect with success'.

In the above example, Step 3 can act as a bridge between the remedial position of focusing on doubts, fears and objections, and the process of connecting emotionally and energetically with success.

We can't emphasise enough the importance of giving some time to the process of positive manifestation through the 'Connecting with Success' process.

So, let's do it again now — describe the territory of success. Write it down, draw it, say it, do whatever you need to do to get that blueprint and start to lay down some new physical, emotional and energetic pathways. Do a few minutes of tapping on the idea and feeling of being there, doing that, having that, being that kind of person. As you tap, mentally step into the future image and focus on it from within the experience looking out, feeling how it will feel when it is real. If you want to repeat something to yourself, have your words be a description of what it looks and feels like being there — what life is like in that future reality — and describe it exactly how you want it to be as you tap on each of the points.

As you do this, you'll be treating your attachment to a previous reality in which this goal did not exist, and making it easier for yourself to feel comfortable in a new reality that you are consciously bringing into form.

What is happening is that you are literally 'getting comfortable' with the idea of being successful, removing the barriers and allowing yourself to open up to the attractive creative force that enables success to happen.

Eventually, the world always becomes 'as you see it'. As you treat yourself for seeing the world anew, and as you start to live in that place, the world will quite literally transform before your eyes.

Once you have set a new goal, action is going to be necessary to achieve it. That action, when you begin, is going to be outside your comfort zone, making it uncomfortable to you. The good news is that by using the 'Connecting with Success' process, you become more emotionally comfortable with the idea of 'being there'. So when you do take action, the discomfort, although it may still be present, is typically easier to bear. At this point we recommend tapping as you go.

Take action towards your goal, and tap as you go in order to process the discomfort of moving into new ways of being ...

## WHEN POSITIVE IS NEGATIVE — ACCEPTING YOUR LIGHT

Self-acceptance and peak performance are actually two sides of the same coin. In our respective practices and in our training workshops, we have been focusing a lot of our attention on treating the 'dark side' — those disowned parts of self that cause us so much trouble. However, for many of our clients, and most likely for you as well, the most disowned parts are actually their positive points, their strengths and their brilliance. They have trouble acknowledging — and even recognising — their strengths, even though they easily recognise yet fight against their weaknesses. Their life then becomes a daily battle where they suffer the push–pull of internal conflict between these warring parts (conflicting internal self-definitions) — the 'internal civil war' as Winston Churchill calls it. It is a war that we all must ultimately rise above if we are to live our lives as fully integrated human beings, where all parts of us are allowed to peacefully co-exist.

We have now come to see manifestation and goal setting as the process of bringing into the light the disowned parts of ourselves that are yearning for expression. These parts exist inside us, but their fullest expression is blocked, often due to negative experiences in our formative years. Their suppression in early life, with the resulting fact that we were unable to manifest them fully, has left them clamouring for expression — however, the negative associations we have developed towards them leave us conflicted and suffering the internal push–pull.

Many have said this — it's the person you become in pursuit of your goals that really matters. That person is even now alive within you! And, if you can remove the barriers to the fullest expression of those parts, and allow yourself to be and become this person, then achievement of your goals occurs with ease — without any inner conflict and a great deal less outer conflict. You are almost drawn to your goals. Congruency and alignment allow your energy to flow unblocked in the direction of goal achievement.

Acknowledging your light, your beauty and your strengths may be the greatest personal development experience of your life.

Recently, we have been experimenting with several processes that allow people to get in touch with their positive parts using EFT/SET. We'd like to share just two of them here.

### 'Being' Goals

This process involves identifying the type of person you want to be and become. How would you like to describe yourself?

Imagine that you are that person now. Hold in your mind an image of you being that person and then step into the image (if you do not easily visualise, it isn't necessary to get an image — just sense what it would feel like being there). Tap continually on the energy points while holding in mind the intention of connecting with how it would really feel to be that person. Do some rounds of tapping on 'I AM THAT' or in EFT using the set-up statement, 'Even though I AM that ...' (e.g. 'Even though I am a confident, powerful person, I fully and completely accept myself.'). As you tap, see yourself from within the future you, feeling and behaving as you would feel and behave if you fully embraced that quality. Continue to tap on the energy points while holding the intention to feel the feeling of what it would really be like being in that future place, manifesting that state.

When you start this process you may find there is a great deal of resistance to getting into the desired state. In addition, there will almost certainly be negative 'tail-enders', which is Gary Craig's term for the opposing negative thoughts that arise to tell you that 'You are NOT like that!' This is what you are using EFT/SET to treat.

Persist with the intention to connect with your desired state of being while continually tapping. As you do, you will soon find that you can access the success state more and more easily. What you are really doing is accepting that state as a part of you (it already is!) and allowing it to be.

Ultimately, you may need to do some tapping on past events where you learned that you are not that person, or that you are a different sort of person; however, we recommend you set aside some time to do this later. Use the time instead to stay focused on accessing the success state.

## Qualities You Admire

This process involves identifying some of the people you admire and listing the qualities they have that you admire the most. Realise that you cannot know those qualities without having them yourself. If you have a negative reaction towards accepting this it is because you have disowned these parts of yourself. This is usually due to past significant events where you learned that you are 'not that'.

Do some initial tapping on the idea of 'I have this quality' or 'Even though I have (this quality), I fully and completely accept myself' in preparation for some further tapping on those significant events where you learned you are 'NOT THAT'. If the events where you learned this come spontaneously to mind while tapping, then focus on those past events one at a time and treat them using the 'Tell the Story' or 'Run the Movie' technique. If the events don't easily come to mind, then ask yourself, 'Where did I learn that I am (the opposite of this quality)?' or 'Where did I learn that I do not have this (positive quality)?' Then practise EFT/SET on the memories and emotions that come up.

We recommend you do these exercises often. As you connect with your success states, in that moment, you are successful. And as you connect with your highest states of being on an ongoing basis, and act upon them, you create the conditions to allow the ongoing manifestation of those ways of being in your life.

# Review and Conclusion

In the world of Energy Psychology, these exciting new Energy Techniques mean that many of the anxiety and fear-based afflictions which used to affect you and limit your life can be treated effectively — even by you, with the right guidance. There is little or no known downside to a gentle, simple, safe, natural process of stimulating your own energy system as we teach it.

There are three main innovative strategies in our SET approach:

- continual tapping

- energy 'toning'

- 'grafting' the tapping on top of — or simply adding the tapping to — any problem (as you perceive it).

This approach is thus largely indirect. It emphasises the meridian stimulation and tends to ignore the mind's activities. Here you don't have to think too much, nor be clever, in order to become more emotionally free.

Direct work, where you focus specifically on emotional problems that you want to treat in order to overcome their negative effects, is also very important and there are many essential applications. The areas we have covered in this book are some of the most interesting according to the feedback we have received. While it is easy to set up a controversy over whether to tap directly or indirectly, the real answer is to do both. Only the disputing mind thinks one is better than the other.

One obvious remaining barrier to acceptance is the way these Energy Techniques, and SET in particular, seem too little and trivial to be able to 'deliver the goods'. If it were something that you needed to learn in a remote part of India or China, after rigorous endurance tests from a Master over several years, and cost several thousand dollars, it would get more respect! The power of the results (common to all modern Energy Techniques) speaks for itself when you do it. Our public workshops often run over several days and we hold them worldwide; if SET didn't work we would find that out right away! The truth is that it is most gratifying to share such a potent method as SET.

EFT/SET do 'work'; no one knows just why or how. If the technique is actually a 'body–energy' one, and the negative emotion you feel lives in the body, then the solution might also be in the body. Certainly EFT/SET have the capability to change body processes involved in trauma and hurt. The majority of the effects seem to come from the actual meridian stimulation regardless of how that is done. In SET we have made ways of applying that stimulation very practical and user-friendly.

It is not necessary to believe in tapping for it to work — in fact, we encourage healthy scepticism. Neither can you ignore the powerful role generally of faith and placebo (the *belief* that something will help bring positive results) in the healing process. Endorphins (natural pain-relieving compounds found in the brain) can be stimulated by acupuncture. They are involved in many body and nervous system responses, so they might be playing a role in the results we see when we use a 'cousin' of acupuncture — acupressure (tapping). At this stage in the development of Energy Techniques, who knows? Actually, we both think the Energy Techniques don't normally get their fair share of the placebo response! EFT/SET tend to work even if you don't believe in them. In the first scientifically validated EFT study performed by Steve Wells and his team, most of the participants did not believe that EFT was actually going to help their phobia, yet help it did. with significant improvements for most participants after just 30 minutes of treatment (see page 223 in Appendix 2: Research).

EFT/SET are ideal as self-help for every condition that has a psychological component. They also function as a harmonising force in the 'body–mind', which all seems too good to be true in the modern world of stress. They bring benefits on many different levels, including changing your habitual levels of unconscious tension, modifying the effects of negative attitudes or feelings, and being healthier generally. They can be used for high achievement and conscious planning. Relationships will generally benefit from the reduced stress these techniques bring. If all this does happen for you over time, then it's likely that you will think and feel quite positively indeed about yourself! Try them out as we suggest, and see.

It's worth pointing out the limits of self-help, as so many people blame themselves when they can't do all the psychological 'heavy lifting' alone. Some are seeking the 'one-minute wonder' cure after they read about this happening to a fortunate person in cyberspace. As we've mentioned in this book, it can be very hard, for example, to resolve moderate to severe depression using only tapping by yourself. Why do this at all? Possibly the reluctance to get professional help with a potentially serious problem like depression (or a potentially major problem with your vision, or an abscess) comes from a mistrust of mainstream medicine.

The simple fact that you are not making progress toward relief of your condition is enough to think about getting some kind of help! Most cases of serious psychological trauma do need an expert's input.

And something else to consider is that if you know how to do continual tapping, then you now also have the option to have treatment from a therapist of any persuasion, *since you can do the tapping while involved in the process.* You could use it before, during and after a session, to facilitate the emotional changes. This broadens your options considerably if you do need professional help — including visiting the dentist!

For many years relaxation was a technique you could learn formally. It had been studied extensively, it was simple to teach and learn, and the benefits were manifold. Now, the 'relaxation response' is a happy side effect from doing the tapping, and it is so reliably present when using EFT/SET that we sometimes forget about it. *It just happens automatically while tapping.* Yet, this was once a primary teaching goal for stress management. So, here is progress, exemplified by relaxation in SET, where 'simpler is better'.

In the field of healing, too often there is an artificial division between mainstream and alternative medicine. Why can't you have the best of both worlds? So we are hoping that doctors will consider new techniques like EFT/SET (even though there is little formal research as yet) because of the compelling results. Likewise, natural practitioners can always provide welcome treatments for most medical conditions (even if it is not a definitive treatment for a serious condition). The prerequisite in *both* camps is having an open mind.

We used to think a decade ago that these methods would spread from the professions to the people, but now it seems obvious that popular acceptance worldwide will bring the process into good repute, so professionals will be obliged to consider using something out of the ordinary. This only means that people are more quickly accepting of results that are effectively personal.

Whatever happens in the outer world, the benefits of using tapping (especially continual tapping within SET) will accumulate for you in your 'inner world'.

Always remember: *the best energy technique is the one that you actually use*. Therefore, the only rule is to use SET if you like it. It is our fond hope that you take this technique and give it a vital role in your living activities. And then …

Share it with everyone.

# Appendix 1: Questions and Answers

Q. Do EFT/SET really work?

A. Yes, they do. EFT/SET have been used personally and professionally by many thousands of people worldwide over the past fifteen or so years. The techniques have been scientifically validated several times but much more of this research is needed. They can't be explained by our current paradigms, however, *qi* energy (or the concept of energy generally) is an accepted foundation of acupuncture, Eastern healing practices, in the martial arts, and maintaining health and wellbeing. As more research is conducted on EFT/SET, and the word spreads, we expect the techniques will be increasingly accepted and used alongside such practices.

Q. Are EFT/SET the same as acupuncture?

A. Yes and no. Some of the same points and meridian system are used in EFT/SET, but the results seem to be superior in the treatment areas of anxiety, fear and trauma. You can deliver far more energy-point stimulation using the 'all-purpose acupressure' of continual tapping than an acupuncture session. So you can treat yourself if that is best, without having to know the theory at all.

Q. Is it safe?

A. We can say EFT/SET are benevolent techniques. The empirical results fit in with the primary law of medicine: first, do no harm. If there is a common negative outcome from tapping, we have not discovered it, nor have we found any from our colleagues' experience. Nevertheless, no technique has ever been proven to be '100 per cent safe' because it is being used for a variety of conditions — to help individuals of different temperaments, in the hands of practitioners of differing competence. Possibly the aggressive use of tapping, without rapport, in a disturbed person (a stupid thing to do, anyway) could further upset them emotionally. Is the tapping technique alone responsible for a bad outcome? If so, it must be rare.

Q. Do I have to believe in this tapping approach for EFT/SET to work?

A. No. It works whether you believe in it or not. Often tapping produces the best results in people who think it won't work at all!

Q. Does tapping work for everything?

A. No. There are some conditions where tapping, by itself, doesn't seem to help at all (e.g. the personality disorders, severe depression, psychotic conditions) and some where it should not be used alone unless you know exactly what you are doing (e.g. infections, fractures, eye and vision problems, head or chest pain).

Q. How do I know the tapping is working?

A. The ultimate sign is that when you apply tapping to a difficult situation or problem for you, after treatment your feelings of upset or distress (no matter how you perceive them) are reduced or even absent, even when you try to think about the difficulty as you did before. During the process of applying the technique, you may feel a range of different shifts in energy in your body. Many people will find that they yawn or sigh during the process, which is a reliable indication that energy is shifting, although not everybody experiences this. The most consistent thing people notice is that they feel more relaxed after tapping.

Q. Can I tap with either hand? Or on either side of the body? Or in different directions? Or jump around to any point?

A. Yes. Order and sequence do not matter to the result. Some energy points may appeal to you more than others. The continual tapping may be done with any points (e.g. the face points, if you are in private). The finger points are usually best for discreet tapping in public.

Q. How many times do I tap on each point?

A. Several times. If you are a bit obsessive, exactly eight times. The regular habit is the important thing.

Q. What if I miss the exact tapping point?

A. No problem. It's not like acupuncture. Near enough is good enough as long as you learn the points well initially.

Q. What if I don't like the actual 'tapping' part?

A. Remember that you can just rub the points gently, or just touch each one and breathe into it (like the 'Touch and Breathe' technique from Dr John Diepold). Even imagining doing the tapping will help the majority of people who try this!

Q. What words do I say for my particular problem?

A. You can focus by saying: 'This problem' (and simple variations), but this might get a bit boring. If you want to work directly on a specific problem, we suggest that it is easier (for someone using self-help) to allow the problem to be in your mind the way it appears normally, then just focus on the thoughts and feelings in your body that follow — 'let them come up'. So no words necessarily, but plenty of reactions and associations. It's the tapping that does much of the work, anyway.

Q. I don't know exactly what my problem is — what do I do?

A. This is normal. You are unaware of the roots, beliefs and connections of your problem because you are separated from knowing that intellectually. But how do you know you have a problem? Because of the distress you feel in a situation. Focus on those feelings in the body and tap — it will be productive, even if you don't find out everything about the problem.

Q. I tapped and I still have some of my problem. What have I done wrong?

A. Nothing. It's only what happened. Some problems are bigger than others; some are not going to respond to a small amount of tapping or to self-help alone. But it's likely that there are parts of the problem that you have left untreated. Either keep going with tapping or get some extra help, or both.

Q. My problem has come back — why?

A. The feeling of having the problem is what has come back. Assuming you have a problem that can respond well — and it did — keep going with the tapping because that feeling might be what is now left — the remaining aspects of the problem — that you now need to treat and resolve (you might be nearly over the upset reaction). If you are unsure about things, or make no progress, talk it through with a professional.

Q.   My problem has not responded to tapping at all.

A.   Maybe it won't, if it is just you doing your own treatment. Or some progress was made but you can't notice that because so much of the problem remains. And is it something that will actually respond? Exactly what is it you are treating? How much treatment should you need, anyway? If you don't know, get help.

Q.   Can I use tapping on my partner/friend/child/moody adolescent?

A.   Possibly. Its better to first treat yourself for your concerns about them or their problems, then work out a way to introduce tapping that would be acceptable, and then decide if you can do what's necessary, or whether they will follow through. After all that, remember that they might respond better to an outsider. Most of the benefits relate to regular self-help and if your loved one won't do that, then what have you achieved? Sometimes the positive changes in you are the best advertisement for the technique.

Q.   I'm not convinced. It's all mumbo-jumbo!

A.   This reaction is understandable considering the amazing claims you hear today for miracle cures. Tapping might seem like many discredited, unethical approaches. Although studies have shown it to be effective for some conditions, it is not fully 'scientifically proven' yet (and that is the end of the story for some), and is far outside the comfort zone of many people. It is a new paradigm.

It looks weird enough to provoke strong reactions! Interestingly, both sceptics (who say 'the results are all due to the placebo effect') and healers (who say 'your body–mind can heal') might explain results similarly, but according to their own beliefs. But if the healing actually occurs, then they both agree in the best way! Something powerful must be happening, but it's a mystery. And yet ... if it does work, even if the explanations leave a lot to be desired, what have you got to lose if it's so simple and easy to try for yourself? If the specific results are there for you personally, after having a good introduction to the treatment, then use it! If not, don't.

# Appendix 2: Research

A number of scientific research studies have found Energy Techniques to be effective — and research is ongoing. Most of the studies that have been completed at the time of writing have been conducted on EFT, as SET is a much newer variation. Clinically, however, we have found the results of SET to be essentially the same as EFT, and many thousands of clients and other clinicians have also found this to be the case. We are currently sponsoring several university research projects on SET treatment for conditions such as trauma, test-taking fears, and phobias. As new research is completed, we will post details on our website at www.simpleenergytechniques.com.

This section provides an overview of some of the most interesting scientific research studies on Energy Techniques that have been completed to date.

## SPECIFIC PHOBIAS

This study, conducted by psychologists Steve Wells, Kathy Polglase, Hank Andrews, Harvey A. Baker and Patricia Carrington found that EFT achieved superior results in treating phobias of small animals when compared to a deep breathing treatment. Participants were treated for their phobias in a single 30-minute treatment, and showed significant improvements in approaching their feared animal, as well as reductions in subjective fear and pulse rates. The improvements on four of the five measures were significantly superior for the EFT treatment. At the 6–9 month follow-up, these improvements were maintained. This research was published in the peer-reviewed *Journal of Clinical Psychology*. (S. Wells, K. Polglase, H. B. Andrews, P. Carrington, H. A. Baker 2003, 'Evaluation of a meridian-based intervention, emotional freedom techniques (EFT), for reducing specific phobias of small animals.' *Journal of Clinical Psychology*, 59:9, pp. 943–966.)

A replication study conducted by Dr Harvey Baker and Dr Linda Siegel at Queens College in New York found roughly similar results to the Wells study. They compared EFT to a counselling approach and found EFT to produce superior results. A follow-up over one year later showed the effects of EFT had persisted. (Baker, Harvey A. and Siegel, L., 'One session of emotional freedom techniques is effective for reducing fear of specific animals: A controlled laboratory study.' Paper presented at the second annual meeting of the Association for Comprehensive Energy Psychology, San Diego, May 2001.)

## POST TRAUMATIC STRESS DISORDER (PTSD)

Dr Paul Swingle and his colleagues studied the effects of EFT on car accident victims suffering from post traumatic stress disorder. These researchers found that three months after they had learned EFT (in two sessions) those car accident victims who reported positive changes as a result of EFT showed significant positive changes in their brain waves and in self-reported symptoms of stress. (P. Swingle, L. Pulos and M. Swingle 2005, 'Neurophysiological indicators of EFT treatment of post-traumatic stress.' *Journal of Subtle Energies and Energy Medicine*, 15, pp. 75–86.)

In 2009, Dawson Church evaluated the treatment of post traumatic stress disorder (PTSD) using EFT on eleven combat veterans and their family members. He found that after five days of EFT at 2–3 hours per day, the group no longer scored positive for PTSD, and the severity and breadth of their psychological distress had decreased significantly. Most of these gains held over time. (D. Church 2009, 'The treatment of combat trauma in veterans using EFT (Emotional Freedom Techniques): A pilot approach.' *Traumatology*, March 15:1.)

## PUBLIC SPEAKING FEARS

Schröninger (2004) studied the effects on public speaking anxiety after a 1-hour treatment session of Thought Field Therapy (TFT — the forerunner to EFT and SET). The 48 subjects, who had to give a speech in front of a small audience, showed significant improvement after TFT treatment, including significant reductions in anxiety as measured by standardised tests, as well as less shyness, increased poise, positive anticipation and interest in giving a future speech. Follow-up interviews four months later indicated that the treatment outcomes had held. (Unpublished doctoral dissertation. Union Institute, Cincinnati.)

Psychologists Sharon Jones and Dr Henry B Andrews from Curtin University, Western Australia studied the effectiveness of EFT on public speaking anxiety in treatment sessions of 45 minutes. The sessions were conducted by psychologists at the university's counselling centre. The authors found significant improvements in self-report and subjective levels of anxiety after the EFT treatment. In tracking the results of EFT treatment throughout the session, they found that anxiety was significantly reduced after just 15 minutes of EFT treatment and continued to reduce throughout the treatment session. (Paper presented to a meeting of the Western Australian branch of the College of Counselling Psychologists in March 2001.)

## TEST-TAKING ANXIETY

EFT was compared with progressive muscle relaxation in self-treatment of exam anxiety in a study by Sezgin and Ozcan (2004). Students who were preparing for a university entrance exam were taught to use EFT, and then instructed to apply it three times per week for the next two months, particularly when feeling anxious about a test. The researchers found that EFT produced significant decreases in anxiety — as measured by a standardised anxiety inventory — and the improvements achieved were superior to the comparison treatment group. (Presented at the Sixth Annual Energy Psychology Conference, Toronto, Ontario, Canada, 2004.)

## EPILEPSY

In a study of children diagnosed with epilepsy, Swingle (2000) found significant reductions in seizure frequency in this group as well as extensive clinical improvement in the children's EEG readings, after exposure to two weeks of daily in-home EFT treatment. (P. Swingle, 'Effects of the emotional freedom techniques (EFT) method on seizure frequency in children diagnosed with epilepsy.' Paper presented at the annual meeting of the Association for Comprehensive Energy Psychology, Las Vegas, Nevada, 2000.)

## LONG-TERM PSYCHOLOGICAL SYMPTOMS

Jack Rowe conducted a study measuring the effects on long-term psychological symptoms after participation in an EFT workshop. Results on the psychological assessment filled out by participants before the workshop, after the workshop, and again six months later showed 'a statistically significant decrease (p < .0005) in all measures of psychological distress from pre-workshop to post-workshop, which held up at the six-month follow-up.' (J. Rowe, *The Effects of EFT on*

*Long-term Psychological Symptoms.' Counselling and Clinical Psychology Journal*; Sept 2005, Vol. 2, Issue 3, pp. 104–111.)

## FIBROMYALGIA

This randomised control trial examined the effects of a self-administered EFT treatment program via the Internet on women diagnosed with fibromyalgia. The trial found significant improvements compared to a waiting list control group on variables such as pain, anxiety, depression, vitality and several other health-related quality-of-life issues. It concluded that EFT seems to be a good complement to other treatment and rehabilitation programs offered to sufferers of fibromyalgia. (G. Brattberg 2008, 'Self-administered EFT (Emotional Freedom Techniques) in individuals with fibromyalgia: A randomized trial.' *Integrative Medicine: A clinician's journal*; August/September, Vol. 7, Issue 4, pp. 30–35)

## SPORTS PERFORMANCE

A study was conducted by Dawson Church (2008) with elite athletes at Oregon State University. This was a randomised double-blind controlled trial with basketball players measuring free throw percentages and vertical jump height. Results showed large gains for those using the Energy Psychology techniques (in this case EFT), who did significantly better than the control group after just 15 minutes of treatment! (This paper was presented at the annual meeting of the Association for Comprehensive Energy Psychology in Albuquerque, New Mexico, in May 2008.)

## ANXIETY

The largest study yet conducted on Energy Techniques was a series of preliminary clinical trials involving more than 29,000 patients from eleven allied treatment centres in South America, which were conducted during a fourteen-year period. A variety of studies were conducted, the largest of which, conducted over a five-and-a-half year period followed the course of treatment of approximately 5000 patients diagnosed with anxiety disorders. These patients were randomly assigned to either an Energy Psychology treatment which used energy-point tapping (as in EFT and TFT), or a control group using Cognitive Behaviour Therapy (CBT) supplemented by medication as needed, with half of the patients (2500) ending up in each treatment. Interviews at the end of the treatment, and follow-up interviews at one, three, six and twelve months, showed that the energy therapy treatment was significantly more effective than the CBT/medication protocol in both the proportion of patients who showed some improvement and the proportion of patients who showed complete remission of symptoms.

Brain mapping studies conducted by Dr Andrade and his team revealed some very interesting findings. They showed that subjects with generalised anxiety, whose acupuncture points were stimulated in the treatment, showed a pattern of wave normalisation throughout the brain and that this both persisted and became more pronounced at the twelve-month follow-up. More details of this study are provided in: Joaquin Andrade, MD and David Feinstein PhD, 'Energy Psychology: Theory, Indications, Evidence' in David Feinstein, *Energy Psychology Interactive*, Innersource, 2004.

## CURRENT RESEARCH

A great deal more research on EFT/SET is currently underway with studies being conducted throughout the world. For example, one controlled scientific study of SET completed at the time of writing found significant improvement in exam anxiety levels experienced by students following a 2-hour SET training session and two weeks of daily practice. Although there is much research yet to be done, these preliminary results, coupled with the clinical reports of many thousands of therapists and the anecdotal reports of many more thousands of members of the public, suggest that these Energy Psychology techniques may represent a major advance in our treatment of emotional distress.

## WHERE YOU CAN FIND MORE INFORMATION ON ENERGY PSYCHOLOGY RESEARCH

The Association for Comprehensive Energy Psychology (ACEP) funds and supports research in this area and has a research committee and co-ordinator. Visit their website at www.energypsych.org for an update of current research and details of international conferences.

David Feinstein has published an excellent overview of current research in: 'Energy Psychology: A Review of the Preliminary Evidence' published in the journal *Psychotherapy: Theory, Research, Practice, Training*, 2008, 45:2, pp. 199–213. A summary of this research overview is provided at his website: www.innersource.net. You can also search on the term 'energy psychology research'.

We provide links to research and resources on our website at www.eftdownunder.com and www.simpleenergytechniques.com.

# Appendix 3: Related Energy Techniques

## THOUGHT FIELD THERAPY (TFT)

EFT owes its origin to this energy therapy, which also involves tapping on energy points. This is the original approach developed by clinical psychologist Roger Callahan. It offers a series of tapping sequences for specific problems — and trained therapists can diagnose particular points of disruption in the energy system and the sequences for treatment. You can find more information at: www.rogercallahan.com.

## BE SET FREE FAST (BSFF)

This advanced energy therapy was developed by clinical psychologist Dr Larry Nims. The letters are an acronym for Behavioural and Emotional Symptom Elimination Training For Resolving Excess Emotions (of) Fear, Anger, Sadness, and Trauma. In the original version, BSFF involved tapping on various energy meridian points, while also directing the subconscious mind to address emotional roots and beliefs associated to the problem being treated. Since 1999, Dr Nims has used a technique that relies entirely upon instructing the subconscious mind to carry out the treatment — and to do so whenever a cue word is used. You can find more information at: www.besetfreefast.com.

## TAPAS ACUPRESSURE TECHNIQUE (TAT)

This wonderful mind–body healing technique was developed by Acupuncturist Tapas Fleming. It involves holding specific acupressure points in a particular pose while addressing several aspects of the problem being treated. It produces excellent results for allergic conditions as well as emotional issues such as trauma. You can find more information at: www.tatlife.com.

# Appendix 4: Further Reading

**PUBLICATIONS**

Dr D. Lake and S. Wells, *New Energy Therapies: Rapid change techniques for emotional healing*, 2nd edn, Waterford Publishing, 2003.

This manual is for helping professionals and provides an overview of some of the key Energy Techniques and Energy Therapies including EFT, BSFF and TAT. It will inform your practice with advice and suggestions from some of the key developers and practitioners of these new techniques. It is a practical resource that will enhance your use of these techniques. Available from: www.eftdownunder.com.

J. Wiese and S. Wells, *Rose and the Night Monsters*, Waterford Publishing, 2004.

This beautiful picture book offers a gentle way of introducing EFT to young children. The exquisite photographic illustrations help children identify with the main character, Rose, as she learns this very simple and user friendly 'tapping' technique to help her overcome her night-time fears. Special guidelines are included for parents, teachers and counsellors for using this new 'psychological acupressure' technique to assist young children to overcome common emotional upsets. Available from: www.eftdownunder.com.

## WEBSITES

**www.eftdownunder.com** and **www.simpleenergytechniques.com**

The best resource for more on the Energy Techniques in this book, these websites include a great deal of information on both EFT and SET, as well as information on the more advanced Provocative Energy Techniques (PET) developed by Steve Wells and Dr David Lake. There are many free articles and tips, as well as the international teaching schedule of the authors.

**www.emofree.com**

The EFT website by Gary Craig. This site is an excellent resource with many pages of information on EFT and its application in treating a wide range of problems. There is also a practitioners' referral list, workshop listing, and links to related techniques and resources.

## TEACHING SEMINARS

Steve Wells and Dr David Lake regularly run practical workshops on Energy Techniques worldwide, for professionals and members of the public. For details on any of their programs and a current workshop schedule, please visit www.eftdownunder.com and www.simpleenergytechniques.com.

## REFERRALS TO PRACTITIONERS

To locate a practitioner trained in Energy Techniques, see www.eftdownunder.com.

# About the Authors

Steve Wells and Dr David Lake are internationally recognised as innovative leaders and skilled practitioners in the new field of Energy Psychology. Steve is a psychologist, professional speaker and peak performance expert from Perth, Western Australia. Dr David Lake is a medical practitioner and psychotherapist in private practice in Sydney, Australia.

David and Steve have been using and teaching Energy Psychology techniques for the past twelve years, and have together developed their own unique advanced integrative energy approach Provocative Energy Techniques (PET), as well as the simplified, user-friendly self-help approach they call Simple Energy Techniques (SET).

*'Every new movement has a number of pioneers who become stars. Steve Wells and David Lake qualify in both regards ... These delightful gentlemen combine wit, humor, skill and compassion in a unique way that both entertains and informs ... It has been my personal pleasure to watch their skills multiply throughout their worldwide audiences.'* – Gary Craig, creator of EFT.

Steve has extensive experience in applying Energy Techniques to peak performance enhancement and regularly consults and presents worldwide with elite athletes and corporate personnel to improve their performance and enhance the performance of their teams. Steve has recently developed a unique program called 100% YES!® which applies powerful Energy Techniques to release the emotional barriers to being able to go for your goals 100 per cent.

David has extensive experience in the treatment of trauma and depression, and also has significant experience in working with relationship issues. His unique relationship approach assists couples to gain freedom from hurt feelings, and has helped many couples to reconnect and rediscover their reasons for being together.

David and Steve have together co-authored three books on Energy Psychology techniques, including *New Energy Therapies*, *Pocket Guide to Emotional Freedom*, and *Tapping Wisdom*. David is also the bestselling author of *Strategies for Stress* and the relationships manual *She'll Be Right*. Steve is also co-author (with Jo Wiese) of a children's book on EFT titled *Rose and the Night Monsters*.

Steve and David have helped thousands of people through their worldwide seminars and workshops. Their workshops and training sessions are entertaining and engaging and filled with practical techniques to improve your life. Their special blend of humour and compassionate provocation also means that their workshops are full of therapeutic fun and laughter while at the same time dealing with deep issues.

Steve and David can be contacted by email at: info@eftdownunder.com.

For more information on Steve and David and their programs visit: www.simpleenergytechniques.com.

# Index

**W**

**Y**

**Z**

**T**